Praise for *The Retirement Income Shift*

Important Insights, Real Solutions. I know that my friend and colleague, Tim Sparks, has the drive, discipline, and passion to help his clients understand how to really take charge of their finances and achieve their retirement goals. Tim also has a natural gift for communicating complex ideas and information in an engaging, down-to-earth way that makes them easy to grasp. I promise you will recognize and appreciate this gift for yourself as you read Tim's book, *The Retirement Income Shift*. You will also learn about Tim's expansive knowledge of investing and the financial markets, along with his candid insights into Wall Street and the dangers of many commonly held beliefs about retirement planning. In his new book, Tim shares solutions he's been using for fifteen years to help hardworking Americans confidently achieve or exceed their financial goals by making "the retirement income shift."

— DAVID J. SCRANTON, CFA®, CFP®, CHFC®, CLU®

Founder, Sound Income Group; Author of *Return on Principle: 7 Core Values to Help Protect Your Money in Good Times and Bad* and *Retirement Income Source: The Ultimate Guide to Eternal Income*

For the first time working with a financial advisor, I feel confidence and trust in leaning on the advice received. Tim takes the time to understand my individual financial situation and goals and takes even more time to educate me in a way that I can rest assured that my finances are in good hands. I simply do not brood over the state of the economy or world as it relates to my financial future. Tim has put those concerns to rest, and I am finally at peace with my investments.

—DR. JAMES L. BORDERS, MD

I would wholly recommend Tim Sparks. Tim has been my financial advisor for a number of years now and has been absolutely brilliant. He has guided me through developing my retirement financial plans including the setup of my retirement paycheck once I hang up my long-time career using the income method. In summary, he has made my money successfully work hard for me.

The income method of generating a retirement paycheck has worked out brilliantly for me. The concept of generating income from your portfolio is an old theme—but rarely is it actually used in today's go-go market. Most people just try to artificially generate income through selling shares, which eventually leads to reverse dollar cost averaging by selling more shares when the market is down. This is devastating to [the goal of] ensuring that you do not run out of money in retirement. Stick with a proven way to generate long-term income by buying income-producing investments. This method just simply works!!!!!!

—JOHN MCNEW, MINING ENGINEER

I had my portfolio with one of the major financial advisory firms and did not feel that they were managing my portfolio in a manner that would have me ready for my planned retirement in six to eight years. Their focus was on mutual funds for growth and continued to assure me that I had time to recover from any downturns in the market, despite my concerns. I usually listened to their radio show on Saturdays while cutting grass and one Saturday I switched stations and Tim's show was on.

After listening to his show, I realized that his information regarding retirement and retirement income, especially the "I" part of the "TR" formula, was the retirement planning method I was looking for instead of "it will grow and you'll be OK" advice that my former financial advisor provided. I called in and set up an appointment and the rest is history. We met with Tim, listened to his recommendations for our retirement plans, went over his projections with him, and realized that his advice and plan fit exactly into our retirement plans. We transferred our portfolios to Tim's group and have been with him for over four years and could not be happier; our portfolios are generating the level of income as projected and, since I have not retired yet, the returns are being reinvested. In addition to not only being the best financial advisor that we have had over our careers, Tim has also become a close friend.

—MIKE CASTLE, JD & ENGINEER

THE
RETIREMENT
INCOME
SHIFT

THE
RETIREMENT
INCOME
SHIFT

GETTING THE MOST MILEAGE
OUT OF YOUR MONEY

TIM SPARKS

Advantage | Books

Published by Advantage Books, Charleston, South Carolina.
An imprint of Advantage Media.

ADVANTAGE is a registered trademark, and the Advantage colophon is a trademark of Advantage Media Group, Inc.

Printed in the United States of America.

10 9 8 7 6 5 4 3 2 1

ISBN: 978-1-64225-924-7 (Hardcover)
ISBN: 978-1-64225-923-0 (eBook)

Library of Congress Control Number: 2024916059

Book design by Megan Elger.

This publication is designed to provide accurate and authoritative information in regard to the subject matter covered. It is sold with the understanding that the publisher is not engaged in rendering legal, accounting, or other professional services. If legal advice or other expert assistance is required, the services of a competent professional person should be sought.

Advantage Books is an imprint of Advantage Media Group. Advantage Media helps busy entrepreneurs, CEOs, and leaders write and publish a book to grow their business and become the authority in their field. Advantage authors comprise an exclusive community of industry professionals, idea-makers, and thought leaders. For more information go to **advantagemedia.com**.

This book is for all of our valued clients, those we've served for many years, and who have entrusted their financial lives to our care.

Also, this book is for those who are entering retirement and want to increase the odds of not outliving their money and get it right, and for those who are in retirement who want their financial well-being to end well.

CONTENTS

Money isn't everything, but it sure does make a good down payment on life.

−WILLIAM BARTLEY, MY STEPFATHER

A WORD FROM THE AUTHOR

My dad has a way of cutting through the noise to focus on what is really important, as demonstrated in the opening quote. He knows there is more to life than money. But he also knows that anyone who says money isn't important either has so much they don't know what to do with it or has never lived without it.

This book is about positioning yourself to make sure you have the money you need throughout your lifetime by positioning your portfolio for your current stage of life.

It is about letting the wisdom of math and logic help assure a comfortable retirement that lasts as long as you do. It's about setting goals for the retirement stage of life and using a conservative yet dynamic strategy to align your investments to reach those goals. It's about transitioning from one stage of life to another. But maybe more than that, it's about change. This shouldn't be surprising, given that life is about change. Yet it always surprises me how many people don't realize that a humongous change in lifestyle—going from working to retirement, going from earning a paycheck to providing your own— also requires an equally humungous mindset change regarding how they manage their money.

Much of the resistance to change is simply inertia. If something has been working—and for most of the people I see, their investment strategies to build a portfolio have been working—it's hard to rally the energy and incentive to change. Even when we *logically* know we should change our investment strategy because our goals have changed, it's hard. Humans are creatures of habit. We simply like consistency and the comfort of the status quo.

Many of us like to think that we would absolutely change our investment style if someone presented sound, sensible reasons to do so. After all, we are all rational people ... right? Why wouldn't we change if it is in our best interest?

Turns out that change is not that easy, no matter who you are. Consider the following:

Several years ago, the Dutch government decided to shut down nearly a third of livestock farms in order to halve the country's overall nitrogen emissions by the end of the decade.[1] But the farmers wanted nothing to do with the government's plans and went on a full-scale disruption of the country's political climate. Their protests included blockading roads, trucking cows to the parliament, and dumping manure on streets to literally cause a stink to show their disapproval. The farmers contended they were protecting not just their land and livelihood but also a way of life passed down from previous generations who had tilled the land. However, Green activists were just as resistant. They quoted scientific evidence to argue that the agricultural sector, and in particular animal husbandry, needed urgent reforms to halt climate change and preserve the environment. While I would not take sides in this debate, this has also been a hotly contested topic throughout the United States and in other countries. My point is that change—no matter what it involves—is rarely embraced by all parties.

---

1   The Guardian. "Netherlands Proposes Radical Plans to Cut Livestock Numbers by Almost a Third." Last modified September 9, 2021. Accessed June 1, 2023. https://www.theguardian.com/environment/2021/sep/09/netherlands-proposes-radical-plans-to-cut-livestock-numbers-by-almost-a-third.

Let's make this a little more personal. How often do we make New Year's resolutions to get in better shape? Probably every year. We might sign up for a gym membership, buy a new cookbook of healthy meals, and maybe even buy a new bike with all the intentions in the world to eat healthier and become more active. But more likely than not, the gym membership goes unused, the cookbooks are never opened, and the bike sits in the garage.

Most of us fall back on old habits simply because we are comfortable with them, and we don't take the time to learn new ones. But if we dig in and get over the discomfort, the results are often well worth it. We can live a more secure retirement. We can shoot free throws underhanded. We can get in better shape. We can live a better life all around. In fact, the path that brought me to this point in my life has been full of change, though it hasn't been easy.

■ ■ ■

Going back to my high school days, I knew I was good at working with people. I knew I thrived in situations that challenged me to excel. I knew I liked learning everything I could about subjects that interested me and then applying that knowledge to solve real-world problems. What I didn't know was what kind of job played to these strengths. My first career position was working as a business-to-business salesperson. I was good at it, but I wasn't really interested in it. It was just a job that paid the bills. I probably should have moved on sooner, but I stayed ten years. Change is hard.

In the late 1990s, I had a chance to get into the mortgage broker business. The country was just coming out of the savings and loan (S&L) banking crisis, during which a third of all S&Ls failed, and the mortgage industry was reinventing itself to avoid similar future disasters. It was an industry that would allow me to use my math and people skills to help buyers find the best financing for the largest purchase they were likely to ever make. Through my skills and client service, I could help people rebuild trust in a process that many had learned to fear. I learned everything I could learn about the mortgage industry. It was a much better fit for my interests, but it wasn't long before I realized the challenge was gone. I was good at it. I had an office of fifteen or twenty loan officers, and my business was flourishing. But I wanted to do more.

People who use a mortgage broker often have unusual financial situations that make it harder to qualify for a traditional mortgage. They might have more debt than normal. They might have poor credit. They might be self-employed. They might have gaps in their job history. When dealing with these clients, I found I was more drawn to helping people manage their debts and/or improve their credit than sourcing the best mortgage for their situation. In fact, I began to look forward to the "debt-challenged" clients because I could do more for them than just source a mortgage.

One day in 2005, a colleague suggested I look at a book he had just read on the financial planning industry. He knew I wanted to do more than mortgage brokering—and that I was already helping clients with more than just their mortgage debt—and thought financial planning might fit the bill. The book was really thick and sat on my shelf for three months before I finally got myself in the mood to tackle it. But once I started, I read the whole thing in two days. It is no exaggeration to say that it changed my life. I was so enthused by the way the author approached the subject that I signed up for several courses—some of them pretty expensive—that gave me additional insights into the industry as well as strategies to provide superior service to clients. I viewed the cost of those courses the same way I viewed investing in a retirement fund. I wasn't buying a new car or taking a luxury vacation. I was investing in my future, my family's future, and the future of my clients.

As I took more classes and talked to planning professionals, I just knew I had found my place. This was a career that allowed me to focus on helping people. It was an industry that was always trying to improve, so I could always be learning. It was a career that would use logic, math, and wisdom to achieve measurable results. I was so sure that financial planning was what I was meant to do in life that I gave up the mortgage business to focus on planning. I put my family's financial health at risk—there were some tough times as I made the transition because I was definitely lacking in cash flow—but I had a goal, and I knew this was the career I was meant to follow.

As hard as that transition was, it gave me a real-world lesson in the importance of cash flow. I had a few real estate assets that made my net worth look attractive, but you can't pay the bills with assets. Without a steady income during those start-up times, we struggled with everyday bills. It's a lesson that seems obvious, yet it's often overlooked in the pursuit of growth. It's not that growth isn't important—it is—but telling the power company that your portfolio grew 14 percent in the past twelve months isn't going to keep the lights on.

Cash flow is crucial, whether you're still in your career phase or in retirement. It's not about growth. It's not about safety. It's about cash flow.

■ ■ ■

Most people have focused on growth since they put that first fifty dollars in a company-sponsored 401(k) plan in their twenties. And focusing on growth has probably served them very well over the past few decades. But as you enter retirement, you need to change tactics. Now you are taking money out rather than putting it in. *Your goals are different, so your solutions need to be different.*

I will dive deeper into statistics and figures in the first chapter on retirement, but needless to say, a large segment of the population is short of cash during at least part of their retirement years, even those with 401(k) plans, pensions, and Social Security. It doesn't have to be that way.

I work with my clients to meet their cash flow needs, all while continuing to see growth in their portfolios. Yes, it's possible to do both. In fact, you *need* to do both. It doesn't have to be an either/or strategy. Too often an advisor's primary solution to providing more income is to utilize bond funds and annuities. Although this may help in the short term, the retiree loses buying power to inflation in the long term. On the other hand, many advisors encourage the retiree to continue to utilize the same growth-based strategies that have been successful during their working years. The problem with this advice is that equities go up and down—and the retiree may have no choice but to sell during a down time if selling stocks is how they are funding their cash flow needs. You don't have to give up growth for cash flow. But you definitely shouldn't give up cash flow for growth. This book will explain in detail how a hybrid approach that combines traditional income strategies with dividend-paying equities for growth works better for nearly all retirees than choosing to focus on one or the other.

I believe so much in the income-plus-growth strategy that I have a weekly radio show where I explain to listeners how they can be more secure in retirement. It's my way of reaching more people than I can on a one-on-one basis in my office. This book is an outgrowth of that desire to reach as many people as I can.

■ ■ ■

I'm reminded of the story of the father and daughter who are spending a day at the beach. As they walk along the path through the dunes, the little girl asks if she can run ahead. The father is bogged down with beach gear and agrees. When he reaches the beach, he sees his daughter standing at the water's edge throwing starfish into the ocean. He asks what she is doing.

"The tide is going out, and the starfish stranded on the beach will die. I'm throwing them back in the water to save them."

The dad looked around and saw hundreds of starfish stranded on the beach.

"That's a great idea, honey, but there are so many. You can't save them all."

"I know," said his daughter as she picked up another starfish. "But I can save this one."

That's how I feel about my investment message. I can't reach everyone. But I can reach many through my practice, my radio show, and this book. If learning a better way to invest during retirement provides more security for even one person who wouldn't have lived as well without that message, I will have done my job.

So, let's get started. By the time you reach the book's conclusion, you will have achieved the following:

- Come to understand how to use the Income + Growth = Total Return equation to make your investments last a lifetime.

- Learned how to use math and logic to determine the best investments for your specific needs.

- Learned why commonly accepted investment maxims shouldn't be so commonly accepted.

- Been provided with specific strategies to make sure you have enough income in retirement to live the life you want to live.

Some of the things I'm going to present will go against everything you've heard. But if everything you've heard was right, there wouldn't be so many people struggling in retirement. Once you understand the process, I have no doubt you'll see the wisdom in it, the same way I did when I read that big, thick book.

As my dad likes to say, "A mind is like an umbrella. It works better when it's open."

With that in mind, let's begin at the beginning. As you read through this book, keep your vision of your retirement years in mind and what you need to keep it on track.

Here's to your successful retirement planning!

Tim Sparks

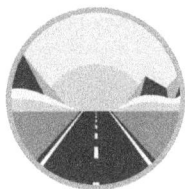

INTRODUCTION

This book is for both the preretiree who wants to get it right before they go into retirement and for the retiree who is already in retirement and wants guidance on how to prevent running out of money before the end of their life. The point of this is to give all retirees an advantage to defy the status quo by not succumbing to all-too-common advice given by way too many financial advisors.

Everything I've read in financial studies still says the number one concern for a retiree is running out of money before the end of their lives. The truth is that you don't want to run out of money, but you may be doing things that can cause you to run out of money. And I'm here to tell you that it's not all your fault ... it's mainly the fault of the financial industry and the "herd mentality" advice that financial advisors espouse. No one in the industry wants to change the philosophy of investing that has been preached for decades. You read about it online. You hear about it in practically every financial advisor's office. All of which leads you to believe that if it's the norm, then you can feel comfortable following the advice you're given.

However, think about this. It took you thirty to forty years to scrimp and save as well as many sacrifices in building your nest egg so you could retire comfortably and stress-free. Do you really think that following the "herd" will preserve your income throughout your retirement?

What you'll learn in this book is that your hard-earned money (your principal) is now being used up faster than it took to build it. Which leads to my second question: Are the reasons given in the financial studies of running out of money legitimate? I think so.

Generally, there are three reasons that people save for retirement, so ask yourself these questions:

- Did you save so you can make a lump-sum purchase like a second home or an RV?

- Did you save so you can leave a large legacy to your children?

- Did you save your money so you can replace those paychecks you received throughout your work life?

I'm willing to bet that the latter is what you chose.

If that's the case, then how do you generate income from your 401(k), a Roth IRA, or brokerage accounts instead of drawing down on the balance? That's your first challenge when you look for the right financial advisor. You are going to hear countless ways to create income while you're *building* your portfolio; unfortunately, there are only two ways you will *get* income from your portfolio once you retire. The first way, and the most common, is engineering income by taking withdrawals from your assets. If you think about it, you can call each withdrawal a set amount of income for you to spend as needed. You can set these withdrawals on autopilot to be paid to you monthly. The question is this: Where is the income coming from?

The second way—and the reason I'm motivated to write this book—is to follow the road less chosen. I know that to be true because I've analyzed over fifteen hundred portfolios over the last fifteen years, and very seldom is what seems to be true income *really* true income. What constitutes true income is your ability to live off the interest and dividends earned from your principal, which pays you three to four times more income than the first way.

Does that mean you're leaving money on the table? Yes! The money left on the table is your principal. Does that mean you're taking more risk? No, not at all, because this is about investing forward in order to have a reliable return based on interest and dividends. Keep in mind that the income you need should be reliable. It's akin to when you were working, when you knew you were going to get paid in regular intervals.

I'm all about preservation of hard-earned assets—those you've earned in your portfolio throughout your work life. That's what the end goal should be. I haven't met anyone who wants to see their retirement balance diminish over time. Imagine if a fiduciary financial advisor, who is supposed to give you pros and cons of particular investment strategies, spent more time on the cons of that conversation. Here's what that conversation would sound like:

"We know the markets change daily. There's a possibility of a few recessions and corrections during this thirty-year retirement plan we are establishing. This means that during those years, if you truly want to preserve principal, then you'll have to cut back on taking withdrawals. As a matter of fact, you may not be able to take *any* income."

Well, at least the fiduciary is telling you what's in your best interest, since your goal is to preserve. They know that markets will come back. But keep in mind that you also have another problem: you need income. You can't pause your bills. And you can't slow down inflation, which impacts everything you buy. This literally means you'll have to sacrifice time, which always seems shorter in retirement. This is no solution!

Here's the sixty-thousand-foot view.

You have two brothers, both of whom have $1 million in retirement savings, and both need $40,000 per year to enjoy life. Brother A is choosing one philosophy for income from his advisor, while brother B is choosing a different philosophy for income from another advisor. Both advisors have committed to getting the brothers $40,000 per year. Brother A's advisor uses a spreadsheet to look at past historical evidence of what the markets have done. This advisor states that the markets typically do x, y, and z, so Brother A's portfolio will last X number of years. On the other hand, Brother B's advisor is more income focused and uses an "income first" allocation model, therefore minimizing the worry about what market history may or may not do. In other words, this advisor doesn't want to trust their own crystal ball.

Fast-forward, and both brothers are retired at sixty-five years of age. The brothers decide to compare their balances and performances over the past ten years to see who chose the best philosophy and, more importantly, the best advisor behind those philosophies. Both were invested in the stock market with a fifty-fifty combination of stocks and bonds.

During the ten-year period, neither brother could have known there would be a five-year drought in the market—i.e., a recession— during which time there was no growth in their portfolios. However, during the other five years, the markets trended upward, but at the end of the ten-year period, the brothers had vastly different results. While they both had $40,000-per-year incomes, the philosophy for Brother A yielded a surprising negative result compared to Brother B: Brother A's balance was reduced to $650,000 whereas Brother B's balance held at $1 million. The difference between the two philosophies equates to the effects of investing for income versus taking withdrawals and calling it income.

How's that possible?

I wrote this book to answer that question. So, turn the page to find out what I'm talking about.

The number one fear for American retirees is running out of money before they run out of breath.

—CERULLI ASSOCIATES[2]

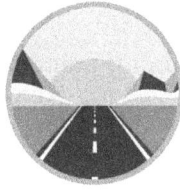

CHAPTER 1

RETIREMENT—IT'S ALL ABOUT INCOME

n 2011, I began working with a client who should have been living his best life. He had entered retirement just ten years earlier with a $1.2 million portfolio, a large family home, a luxury vacation home, and plans to someday leave his children a large estate. He and his wife enjoyed traveling, treating family members to memorable vacations, participating in meaningful hobbies, supporting charities important to them, and hosting the best parties in town. This was the life he had worked, saved, and invested for decades to achieve.

Yet as we looked at his current situation, he was in tears. That $1.2 million portfolio was down to $470,000. There was a very real possibility that if he didn't make some major changes, he would run out of money within a few years. Given that both he and his wife came from families with long lives, he needed that portfolio to perform for more than a few years. He was already looking to sell the second home that held so many wonderful family memories. He was no longer

---

2   Lorie Konish, "Retirees' Biggest Fear Is Outliving Their Assets, Research Finds," CNBC, June 13, 2023, https://www.cnbc.com/2023/06/13/retirees-biggest-fear-is-outliving-their-assets-research-finds.html#:~:text=These%20tips%20can%20help,-Published%20Tue%2C%20Jun&text=As%20saving%20for%20retirement%20has,cohorts%20is%20outliving%20their%20assets.

funding the vacations that brought his far-flung family together each year. He was dreading telling his grandchildren that he wouldn't be able to help with their college expenses. He was humiliated, stressed, and scared.

How did this happen? He had done everything right getting to retirement. Why was it all falling apart?

Granted, he had experienced two of the steepest bear markets in history. But that wouldn't have been a problem if he hadn't been selling his stocks each year to cover expenses. His real problem? His portfolio's actual income component wasn't high enough. He was getting about 1.5 percent ($18,000) income from his investments—this was the average dividend yield for the S&P 500 from 2000 to 2013—and needed almost 5 percent ($60,000) to cover his withdrawals and protect him from market volatility. If he had been achieving 5 percent from his income investments during those first ten years, he would still have his $1.2 million portfolio. Instead, he had been eating into his principal, and when the markets fell, his investments were unable to replace those withdrawals via appreciation. He got to enjoy the first ten years of retirement, but after that he was just surviving.

When I explained how he got into this situation, he was eager to make changes that would increase his investment income. However, it was really too late to completely recover. Using a balanced strategy involving dividend-paying equities plus bonds and bond-like instruments as well as proceeds from the sale of his second home, we were able to achieve a $30,000 annual income stream. This sliced his income in half, but it was better than continuing to whittle away at his assets. It would still require him to significantly downsize his lifestyle—he'd lost his second home and curtailed most of his travel—but now his money would last as long as he needed it.

He and his advisor had relied for too long on the assumption that the market would continue to go up. It didn't. His advisor told him not to worry—the market would come back. And it probably would—it always has—and therefore there was a chance that over time his principal could again grow, but it was going to take several years that he might not have.

In the end, it all boiled down to a failure to change his investment strategy as he entered retirement. It is extremely common for advisors to continue to rely on growth strategies well past the time when they should adjust for the retiree's new reality. *Retirement is all about purpose, not performance.* In retirement, the purpose of a portfolio is to provide cash flow to cover expenses, not build wealth. That is the goal during the working years, when you need a portfolio to perform and grow. People work to build wealth during the accumulation years, and most of my clients do that very well.

It's relatively easy to build wealth when you are receiving a regular paycheck, your employer might be matching savings contributions, and you can ride out—or even take advantage of—down markets. But when you go into retirement, your savings have to carry the baton for twenty, thirty, or more years. In that time, how much volatility will there be? You can't suspend distributions just because the market is down. Bills still need to be paid. Building wealth is easier than keeping wealth.

Thus, retirement is about income. Because you no longer have a regular paycheck, the wealth you've accumulated must generate income for you. What works so well in the accumulation phase of life doesn't typically work in the distribution phase. It might seem obvious, but it needs to be said: *The retirement phase is radically different from the career phase and thus needs a different approach to financing and investing.*

Moving from the accumulation stage of financial investment to the distribution stage is a huge psychological change. You spend decades adding to your portfolios and being rewarded by seeing larger and larger balances at the end of most years. It's what keeps you going. Now, the goal is to preserve that balance by being income focused first and growth focused second. You need to celebrate when the balance remains constant year after year. Instead of watching a balance grow, you need to find your rewards in the cash flow distributed each month or quarter. It's a different way of looking at financial health that many people fail to adjust to.

Now let's look at what factors should be considered when making decisions for an investment strategy that works for retirement.

Length of Retirement

It wasn't that long ago that news shows featured the birthday celebrations of local residents celebrating their hundredth birthday. The *TODAY* show even had a weekly segment where Willard Scott gave national recognition to those reaching that milestone. Celebrating a hundred-year birthday was a rarity, and it certainly felt like national TV congratulations, complete with a picture, were in order. Today, we all know people who are active well into their nineties, and envisioning them reaching the century mark isn't farfetched—or even newsworthy.

According to the Stanford Longevity Center, the perception that more people are living to see their hundredth birthday is firmly based in reality. In fact, in less than a century, the average life expectancy in the developed world has increased by about thirty years.[3] What does

---

3   Stanford Center on Longevity, "About the Center," accessed May 7, 2024, http:// longevity.stanford.edu/about-the-center/.

this mean for you? It means retirement could last a very long time. The average length of retirement is 18.6 years for men and 23.8 years for women, but a large segment of the population spends many more years living on Social Security and their investments.[4] That means the portfolio you enter retirement with will likely need to be recalculated if it is to support a retirement that could conceivably last as long as your career.

Costs in Retirement

Most people are very bad at estimating how much money they will need in retirement. Many are so fearful of running out that they greatly downsize their lifestyle. They buy a small house in a less expensive part of the country. They forgo travel and other entertainment. They essentially cut expenses to the bare bone. This is not the type of retirement most of us want—and if a portfolio is arranged correctly, it's not what most of us need to do.

However, you can't blame people for being cautious. Estimating how much retirement costs is hard, and getting it wrong can have dire consequences. You might have seen the algorithms that suggest you will need about 80 percent of your preretirement income in retirement to maintain your lifestyle. That sounds simple. And it is. Too simple. Retirement isn't a sprint—it's a marathon. Or maybe more accurately, a triathlon, complete with three very different legs.

The first phase of retirement is probably the most expensive. This is the time you are most active. While many retirees are fretting and cutting way down on expenses, countless others are choosing to travel more and for longer times than they were able to do during

---

4   OECD, "Expected Number of Years in Retirement by Sex," accessed June 1, 2023, https://stats.oecd.org/index.aspx?queryid=54758.

their working years. They socialize, eat out at restaurants, engage in expensive hobbies, and often enjoy providing funding for grandchildren's education and adventures. Expenses during this phase can easily surpass those of a preretirement life.

Then we come to the middle phase. If your health is holding up, these could be the least expensive years. Energy levels are often beginning to flag, so many retirees find themselves happy to reduce travel and socializing. They fall into a comfortable routine that tends to revolve around home and family. Living expenses are predictable, while philanthropic and family expenses are manageable. This phase can very easily involve fewer expenses than your preretirement life.

Next, we enter the third phase, which is a wild card. If your health is good, you could be living a quiet life with very few expenses. If, however, you require assisted living, nursing care, or in-home aides—and according to the US Department of Health and Human Services there is a 70 percent chance you will—this can be a tremendously expensive time of life. It is best to hope for the best while preparing for the worst. This is the time you want to have all your principal available, if needed.

It is easy to see that simply aiming for 80 percent of preretirement income is only a rough estimate that could leave you without enough cash flow in one stage and too much in another. To cover costs, you will want to set up a portfolio that provides enough income to cover initial-phase costs while preserving principal in case it is needed later. Thinking 80 percent is good enough at all times in retirement is a recipe for ending up with too little money.

Goals in Retirement

The number one goal mentioned by more people than any other is making sure their money lasts as long as they do. The next goal is leaving a legacy for their children. To accomplish both these goals, as well as any others a retiree might have, the portfolio must be set up to provide enough cash flow to cover expenses while continuing to grow the principal.

You want to cover your needs (food, utilities, insurance, etc.), wants (travel, hobbies, charitable contributions, etc.), and wishes (second home, college expenses for grandchildren, an inheritance for your children, etc.). The mistake many retirees make—often on the advice of their financial advisors—is to either (1) convert growth stocks into cash equivalents, such as Treasury bills, bond funds, and annuities while at the same time taking 4 percent out of their portfolio each year. Or, conversely, (2) leave their portfolio heavily invested in growth stocks, which were never meant to provide income. Both of these strategies might pay for everyday expenses, at least in the beginning, but they will eventually stress a portfolio's principal, making a legacy less likely.

What is needed is a solution that aligns with your retirement goals. That solution usually comes down to a balanced portfolio of dividend-paying stocks along with bond and bond-like vehicles, which will provide income for everyday expenses as well as growth for principal preservation.

EQUITIES VERSUS FIXED INCOME

I tend to see two kinds of new clients. The first group comes to me with a portfolio that is composed primarily of growth stocks, while the second group has gone all in on bond funds, annuities, and other fixed income products. Just as we're always told to never put all our eggs in one basket, putting all your savings in one extreme or the other rarely works out in the end.

Growth stocks are great for building wealth over a long period of time, and many retirees and their advisors look at the results of a portfolio's life and make the decision to continue in growth mode. In fact, their previous advisor likely pointed to the great returns during the past decades and told them they *needed* to stay in these stocks to keep up with inflation and make sure they didn't fall behind. This advice isn't bad—at least over the long term.

But we often have short-term amnesia. On average, the markets have indeed gone up decade after decade. So, we forget about those short but significant downturns. When you were building wealth, those downturns might have caused some concern, but most long-term investors simply held on and came out of them better than ever. Those downturns quickly fade from memory.

Percentage Needed for Recovery

$$Y=X/(1-X)$$
X=percent loss   Y=percent needed

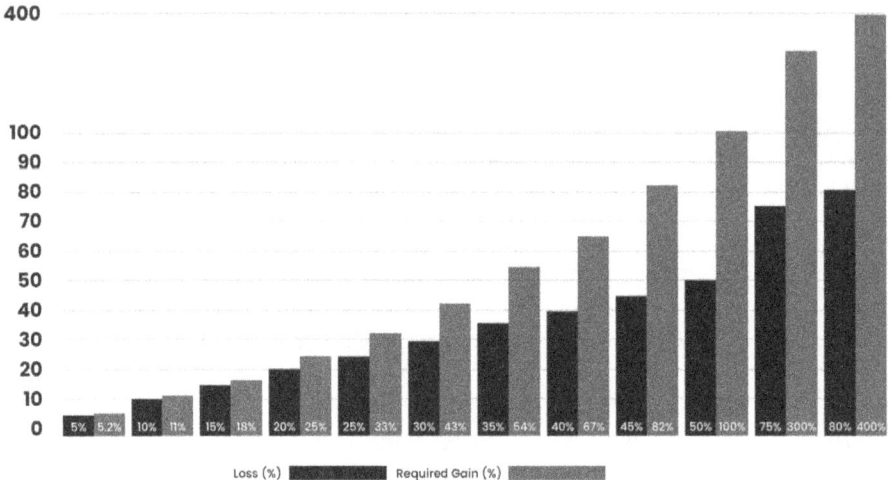

| Loss (%) | | Required Gain (%) | |

| 5% | 5.2% | 10% | 11% | 15% | 18% | 20% | 25% | 25% | 33% | 30% | 43% | 35% | 54% | 40% | 67% | 45% | 82% | 50% | 100% | 75% | 300% | 80% | 400% |

But retirement is different. You can't ride out the downturns because you need those investments to live on. Not only is a falling stock market reducing your net worth on paper but selling stocks to fund your day-to-day living expenses is further reducing principal for real. Your portfolio is getting hit from all sides, and that is hard to recover from because losses have a much greater impact on a portfolio than gains do. The chart on this page illustrates just how large a gain you need to make up for various levels of loss. A small loss doesn't hurt too much. But as the losses increase, it becomes harder and harder to recover. The idea, of course, is to avoid losses if at all possible.

Let's look at a hypothetical example. I'm using rounded numbers to keep it simple. Say you have a $1 million portfolio comprised primarily of growth stocks, and you are redeeming (i.e., selling) $50,000 each year, which in the past has been covered by 5 to 6 percent average returns. Let's say the country enters a two-year bear market and you experience a 20 percent loss. Now your balance is $800,000. You still need that $50,000 per year to live on, so you withdraw $50,000 the first year of the two-year down market, and your portfolio now stands at $750,000. You do the same thing the second year, and you are left with $700,000. This isn't looking good.

But wait … just as everyone predicted, the markets rebound. In fact, they quickly climb 20 percent. However, that 20 percent gain doesn't make up for the 20 percent loss because 20 percent of $700,000 is only $140,000, resulting in a portfolio balance of $840,000.

Now let's look at a different hypothetical. What if, instead of a portfolio of growth stocks, you had a $1 million portfolio of dividend-paying stocks plus some bonds and bond-like instruments, which together provided $50,000 in yearly income, so you did not need to sell stocks to cover your cash flow needs. The market would still have lost 20 percent and your portfolio balance might have fallen to $800,000, but when the market rebounded, you would have regained $160,000 of your loss. Add that to the $800,000, and you end up with $960,000 instead of $840,000. That is quite a gap, and it will only grow greater as the years go on.

Needing to access principal at an inopportune time often creates a downward spiral. We'll go deeper into the numbers and math in a later chapter, but it is often at this point that I find people in my office trying to figure out why they went from a $1.2 million portfolio to a $470,000 portfolio in ten years.

The second group of people I mentioned earlier—the bond fund and annuity group—come to me with the opposite strategy. As they entered retirement, they realized they needed current income, so they converted all or nearly all their equities to fixed income. Their portfolios are now made up almost entirely of annuities, T-bills, bond funds, and other cash equivalents. For the first few years, the income from these investments covered all their needs as well as most of their wants, just as they thought it would. They felt secure and in control.

But as the years went on, they noticed that their cash flow was getting tighter. Everything from food to utilities to entertainment was getting more expensive. Likely their medical outlays were also increasing. Many expected to help with grandchildren's college, weddings, and first homes. That help now looked very unlikely to materialize. In fact, they were beginning to fear they might someday need help themselves from family to cover expenses. Putting their savings into income-producing vehicles was supposed to provide a safe, secure retirement. What was happening?

What happened is, they laid the foundation for a solid investment house but neglected to build the walls and roof to protect that foundation. And it wasn't their fault. Converting equities into fixed income investments as we near retirement is a strategy promoted by everyone from individual advisors to robo-advisors to television personalities. It makes a lot of sense to become more conservative, but a safer strategy requires more nuance. We shouldn't be confusing stable with safe. If your income remains stable while expenses increase, you can't help but fall behind. That would seem to be the opposite of safe.

Advisors make suggestions based on return assumptions going into the future. Unlike many areas of life, where short time frames are easier to predict, return assumptions love long time frames. It's like Tiger Woods back in his prime. You might not have been able to predict exactly which tournaments he would win, but you could be pretty confident that at the end of the season, he'd be number one. Return assumptions are similar. We might not know exactly what they will do next week or next month, but we know they will go up over the long term.

The problem arises when we make investment decisions based on future assumptions without taking into account short-term volatility. The advisor is considering "over time" as their argument for using growth-based mutual funds without regard to recessions or corrections while simultaneously taking withdrawals. Using a growth strategy that doesn't account for short-term market fluctuations—when the goal is long-term preservation—can cause permanent damage to the portfolio.

When making assumptions, the best you can do is put a floor on it. Advisors will suggest bond funds and annuities to ensure you don't lose money if the markets go down, but that's not enough to cover rising expenses. For example, during the past two years, annuities had a zero return. Annuity owners didn't technically lose anything. They didn't lose 20 to 30 percent of their money when the market collapsed, but they didn't make anything either. And as inflation increased, they lost buying power. That is a real loss, even if it doesn't show up on paper.

By this time, you are saying, "OK. You've now convinced me that I don't want a portfolio full of equities or a portfolio full of fixed income. So, what do I want?"

If you are going to keep up with inflation, then you are going to need to increase dividends and interest payments while still protecting your principal. And there is a very good way to do this.

A Better Way

As I mentioned earlier, retirement is all about purpose, not performance. However, you can't completely ignore performance. While the volatility inherent in the equities markets can doom an equities-heavy portfolio, the lack of growth in an income-heavy portfolio can cause its own problems. The solution is to align your portfolio with your new goals. While you previously aimed to grow a nest egg, your goal now is to have the cash flow to fund a comfortable retirement.

Many of the portfolios I see today remind me of a farmer who owns 200 acres. It's all great land, but he has only 20 acres planted. The other 180 acres are sitting fallow. Those acres are undoubtedly going up in value, but they aren't providing income. The only way to take advantage of appreciation is to sell the land, which isn't a sustainable plan. What does he do in a few years when he doesn't have any more land to sell? Instead, he needs to plant those fallow acres and get them working for him.

Stocks should be viewed the same way. When I look at a portfolio, I almost always see several mutual funds, maybe an exchange-traded fund (ETF), and rarely a few individual stocks. Some may be dividend producing, but that is just incidental. They weren't intentionally chosen for that feature. That means the stocks are lying fallow, just like the empty farm fields. They are appreciating, but they aren't working for the retiree. You don't want to rely on appreciation to meet your cash flow needs any more than the farmer wants to rely on selling land to meet his needs.

If you have set up the portfolio to work for you—rather than just passively appreciate—you can hold on to your principal in down markets and benefit in up markets. For example, between 2000 and 2013, the market went thirteen years without appreciation.[5] That was a disaster for a lot of portfolios. But for those set up to provide income via dividends, the principal first remained intact during the dry years and then tripled in value when the markets came back between 2013 and 2021.

That is the portfolio you want in your retirement years.

Now let's dive a little deeper into the world of investments to determine the best strategy for your particular situation. We'll start with investment myths that everyone seems to believe but that can derail even the best-thought-out strategy.

QUICK TAKES

In retirement, your portfolio is not about the assets you save; it's about the income you can get from the assets you saved.

- **Retirement Goal:** Have enough cash flow to fund a comfortable retirement.

- **Roadblock:** Portfolios tend to be too weighted to growth stocks, which need to be sold to create cash flow, or too weighted to income, which loses value to inflation.

- **Solution:** Rebalance the portfolio to include both bonds and bond-like instruments as well as sustainable, dividend-paying equities that provide income to cover expenses plus growth to protect principal.

---

5   Advisor Perspectives. "The S&P 500, Dow, and Nasdaq since Their 2000 Highs." Last modified May 2, 2024. Accessed May 23, 2024. https://www.advisorperspectives.com/dshort/updates/2024/05/02/the-s-p-500-dow-and-nasdaq-since-their-2000-highs. *If you look at these charts, they show no appreciation between 2000 and 2013.

You learn something new every day if you pay attention.

–RAY LeBLOND

CHAPTER 2

BEWARE CONVENTIONAL WISDOM— FIVE MYTHS TO IGNORE

'm all about educating my clients. I want each one to be a true partner with me in their retirement planning. But they can't do that if they don't understand what I am proposing and why I am proposing it. However, when I talk about educating my clients, I often hear, "Why would they possibly need educating? The world is full of financial information—internet blogs, financial services firms' research papers, TV infomercials, aisles and aisles of books—what more do people want?"

What they want and need is *accurate* information. I'd wager that most of what they think they know about investing came from organizations or advisors who have a vested interest in the retiree or soon-to-be-retiree following their recommendations. If a firm sponsors mutual funds, it is likely going to promote mutual funds as the best way to secure your retirement. If it aggregates bond funds, then bond funds become the golden goose. I spend much of my time first disabusing clients of widely held beliefs and then helping them see a better way.

Let's look at a few of the most common myths I encounter on nearly a daily basis. I'm guessing a lot of you will recognize several of them.

MYTH #1: You will need less money in retirement than during your preretirement years.

FACT: Many retirees need as much or more cash flow in retirement, particularly in the early years, than they did in their preretirement years.

While often-stated rules of thumb suggest that retirees will need only 70 to 80 percent of their preretirement income to fund their golden years, this simply isn't the case in many—maybe most—cases. With more time on your hands for the things you love, it's only natural for spending to escalate—especially if you plan on traveling, visiting family members, or pursuing new hobbies and activities. Surveys of retirees have found that many spend as much, or even more, in the early years of retirement than before they retired.[6]

What is even more worrisome is that for those retirees who actually find they can get by on 70 percent of their preretirement income, only 25 percent have a revenue stream from their portfolio, pension, and Social Security that generates that level of income. Meanwhile, more than half of retirees—51 percent—have to make

---

6   "Expenses and Income Needed in Retirement," Wells Fargo, accessed May 7, 2024, https://www.wellsfargo.com/financial-education/retirement/retirement-income-needs/.

do with less than 50 percent of their preretirement income because that is all the income they have.[7]

In other words, they aren't funding their retirement on 70 percent of their preretirement income because that is all it takes to cover their retirement life needs, wants, and wishes. They are funding their retirement life on 70 percent or less because that is all they have, and their lives are not at all what they expected.

It is logical to think that retirement will be less costly than preretirement times. After all, retirement typically eliminates expenses like commuting to work, retirement fund contributions, office wardrobes, and teenagers eating you out of house and home. But overall expenditures may be on the rise. For example, healthcare costs tend to increase with age. And inflation doesn't stop just because your paycheck does.

Another related misconception is that you'll pay less in taxes once you're retired. If you have less income, your taxes will go down, right? But that assumes you'll have less income. If you end up with the same amount of income in retirement as you had when you were working— and, if your financial investment plan worked the way you expected it to, you very likely will—you may not be in a lower tax bracket. As a retiree, you may qualify for fewer tax breaks, such as mortgage and college savings deductions. And of course, tax rates may also rise in the future while your retirement income remains static.

In other words, being able to live the lifestyle you desire on less money than you had before retirement is not a given. Many people do, indeed, live on less income in their retirement years. But it's not because they want to; it's because they have to. Do you really want to

---

7   Lorie Konish, "75 Percent pf Retirees Fall Short of a Key Retirement Income Goal," CNBC, January 21, 2023, https://www.cnbc.com/2023/01/21/retirees-fall-short-on-retirement-income-replacement-ratio.html.

cut back and economize at a time in life when you should be enjoying yourself?

While it's possible that you'll be able to live the retirement of your dreams while spending less in retirement than previously, counting on it can lead to a retirement life that is much less vibrant than you expected. A better plan is to assume you will need to replace your preretirement income and adjust your portfolio to do so.

MYTH #2: You can't go wrong with mutual funds and ETFs.

FACT: In retirement, relying on mutual funds and ETFs is likely to be a principal-reduction strategy.

The majority of advisors as well as employer retirement plans such as 401(k)s and 403(b)s encourage their clients to stick with mutual funds and ETFs throughout their retirement years. Very likely these are the vehicles the advisor used during the accumulation phase, and they are comfortable recommending that the retiree remain with them. Why rock the boat if it's been getting you to where you want to be?

Many advisors also find it hard to let go of mutual funds because they work for financial services firms that sponsor or promote mutual funds and ETFs. The organizations encourage (sometimes require) the advisors in their networks to use the firms' products. The vast majority of these advisors truly believe in their product. But maybe they shouldn't.

These advisors are doing what they think is best for their clients, but they have often succumbed to the "disease of ease." They can simply reach up on the shelf and bundle a group of mutual funds and ETFs that have been vetted (by their sponsoring firm) as appropriate for retirees.

These "retirement-friendly" mutual funds may seem stable, safe, and the perfect way to own stocks in retirement, but they can come with unexpected risks, like the following, for example:

- High Expense Ratios and Sales Charges
  If you're not paying attention to mutual fund expense ratios and sales charges, they can get out of hand. Fees always reduce overall investment returns. When you are building your portfolio, these fees are usually covered by returns. But when you are in the distribution phase, these fees can reduce returns to the point where you need to sell more shares than you expected to cover living expenses and thus reduce your principal more than you expected. This is not a sustainable long-term strategy.

- Tax Inefficiency
  Like it or not, investors do not have a choice when it comes to capital gains payouts in mutual funds. Due to the turnover, redemptions, gains, and losses in security holdings throughout the year, investors typically receive distributions from the fund that are an uncontrollable tax event—sometimes leading to unexpected capital gains taxes.

I look at mutual funds as a "principal-reduction" strategy. If you need your portfolio to produce 4 to 6 percent in income to cover your expenses, you are not going to get that with mutual funds. You will have to sell shares each year to provide the income you need. Add on the annual fees, and you are slowly reducing the size of your portfolio—which often means you will need to sell even more shares the next year to achieve the same income. This is a cancerous strategy that eats away at your principal over time.

A better solution is to use individual dividend-paying stocks and bonds that provide the level of income you need while still providing some growth. This strategy should preserve your principal so that if a time comes when you need to sell assets to cover medical costs, assisted-living expenses, or other emergencies, you will have it. It won't have been eaten away with annual redemptions and distributions.

> **MYTH #3:** The stock market always goes up.
>
> **FACT:** The market has its ups and downs—and those downs are often at the most inopportune times.

Every myth has a kernel of truth … and this one is more than a kernel. The stock market *has* always gone up *over time*—but it has not gone up in a straight line. The following chart illustrates the upward trajectory of the market over the long term, but it also highlights that there have been multiple instances of peaks and valleys in the past 120 years.[8] Investors can ride out the valleys during their working years, but having to sell assets to fund a retirement when the market is down can be disastrous to future security.

People are optimistic by nature. We tend to focus on the good and forget the bad. Baby boomers entering retirement seem to be particularly adept at this. They have lived through bear markets, yet they mostly remember the year-after-year bull markets of the past decade. This has led to an unprecedented capital flow into equities— and unlike previous generations, this generation isn't switching to fixed income as it nears or enters retirement.

---

8   MacroTrends. "Dow Jones – 100 Year Historical Chart." Accessed June 1, 2023.
     https://www.macrotrends.net/1319/dow-jones-100-year-historical-chart.

For example, at Fidelity Investments, nearly 40 percent of investors in the sixty-five to sixty-nine age range hold two-thirds or more of their portfolios in stocks. In taxable brokerage accounts at Vanguard, one-fifth of investors eighty-five or older have nearly all their money in stocks, up from 16 percent in 2012. The same is true of almost a quarter of those aged seventy-five to eight-four.[9]

When I meet with clients, I talk about the importance of using nuance, details, and math to make sound investment decisions for each stage of life. It is a fact that from 1926 to 2023, the stock market had an average annual return of a little over 10 percent, before inflation. When inflation is factored in, the average annual return falls to just under 7 percent.[10] However, this doesn't mean you will realize a 7 percent after-inflation return each year. Some years you might have a 3 percent return and other years a 12 percent return—and some years will result in negative returns.

---

9   Anne Tergesen, "America's Retirees Are Investing More Like 30-Year-Olds," *Wall Street Journal*, July 4, 2023, https://www.wsj.com/articles/it-isnt-just-boomers-lots-of-older-americans-are-stock-obsessed-ca069e1a.

10   "Stock market returns since 1926," Officialdata.org, https://www.officialdata.org/us/stocks/s-p-500/1926#:~:text=S%20percent26P%20percent20500%20percent3A%20percent20%20percent24100%20percent20in%20percent201926%20percent20%20percentE2%20percent86%20percent92%20percent20%20percent241%20percent2C256%20percent2C413.21%20percent20in%20percent202023&text=This%20percent20is%20percent20a%20percent20return%20percent20on,%20percent2C%20percent20or%20percent206.99%20percent25%20percent20per%20percent20year.

Stock Market Ups and Downs 1900–2023

"Dow Jones—DJIA—100 Year Historical Chart," Macrotrends, accessed May 7, 2024, https://www.macrotrends.net/1319/dow-jones-100-year-historical-chart.

While the graph above does indeed confirm that the market always comes back, your portfolio might not. When you are in retirement and taking money out of your portfolio rather than putting it in, you might not have the time to recover. Your principal and balance can easily take a terminal hit during a couple of down years. Even after the market begins to recover, your principal will likely continue to get reduced. Your balance will continue to fall. Your money may not last twenty or thirty years. No wonder everybody's worried they're going to run out of money before running out of breath. They know that believing the market will always go up is too good to be true … because it is.

Retirees need consistent, stable income to pay their bills and live their lives. When they are required to redeem equities during a down market, they end up mortgaging their future needs for current needs.

At this point, it would be logical for you to say, "Well, I guess that means I need to get out of stocks when I'm ready to retire." And that brings us to Myth #4.

MYTH #4: You should move out of stock funds and into bond funds when you retire.

FACT: Individual income-producing stocks and bonds will serve you better than a static portfolio heavy on bond funds.

After debunking Myth #3, you might expect me to advocate for a bond-heavy portfolio. You would be wrong. I advocate for an "income-heavy" portfolio. And here is where we again get into nuance and details.

Advising clients to get out of the equities markets as they near or enter retirement is still a very common strategy. In fact, there is an entire family of funds—target-date funds—that move people along a continuum from mutual funds to bond funds based solely on their retirement date.

This strategy made sense when retirements were shorter and inflation didn't have as much time to erode savings. Planning for a thirty-year retirement, as you should do now, changes the thinking. Now I hear some advisors telling their clients they should keep a percentage of stocks in their portfolio equal to 110 or 120 minus their age. This advice recognizes the fallacy of relying too heavily on bond funds, but it's still wrong.

It's not the number of stocks or bonds you have in your portfolio that makes the difference. It's the *kind* of stocks and bonds you hold. Growth stocks and bond funds will typically not provide the income you need. Instead, a focus on conservative, dividend-paying stocks and select individual bonds (i.e., not a bond fund) is a strategy that should provide the income you need to live on today while protecting principal for higher or unexpected expenses in the future.

MYTH 5: You can take 4 percent of your principal each year and never run out of money.

FACT: This factoid was never 100 percent correct, and in today's economic climate, it can be astonishingly dangerous.

One frequently used rule of thumb for retirement spending is known as the "4 percent rule." It's relatively simple. You add up all your investments and withdraw 4 percent of that total during your first year of retirement. In subsequent years, you adjust the dollar amount you withdraw to account for inflation. By following this formula, you should have a very high probability—85 percent is a level suggested in some writings—of not outliving your money during a thirty-year retirement, according to the rule. (I've always wondered why we don't care about the 15 percent that apparently followed the rule but ran out of money anyway.)

For example, let's say your portfolio at retirement totals $1 million. You would withdraw $40,000 in your first year of retirement. If the cost of living rises 2 percent that year, you would give yourself a 2 percent raise the following year, withdrawing $40,800, and so on for the next thirty years. This rule has been a guiding standard for most retirement advisors since 1994, when it was proposed by researcher

William Bengen.[11] However, recent research by Dr. Michael Finke, Dr. Wade Pfau, and Morningstar researcher David Blanchett determined that by using the US economic data of the twenty-first century for analysis (rather than that of the twentieth century that was used by Bengen), the acclaimed 4 percent rule would have an astounding failure rate of 57 percent.[12]

Even before new research indicated that the 4 percent rule might not be as safe as thought, we were looking at a 15 percent failure rate. That might not seem too bad if you are talking about garden seedlings or college applications. But do you want to be one of the 15 percent that faithfully follows the 4 percent rule and still runs out of money? Would you get on a plane that landed safely only 85 percent of the time? Of course not. You want that plane to work 100 percent of the time. And you want your retirement portfolio providing adequate income as long as it's needed.

While the 4 percent rule could be a reasonable place to start, it doesn't fit every investor's situation. Reasons it might not be right for your situation vary, but a few include the following:

- *It's a rigid rule.*
  The 4 percent rule assumes you increase your spending every year by the rate of inflation—not based on how your portfolio performed—which can be a challenge for some investors. It also assumes that you never have years where you spend more, or less, than the inflation increase rate. Expenses may change from one year to the next, and the amount you spend may

---

11 Wikipedia. "William Bengen." Last modified June 1, 2023. https://en.wikipedia.org/wiki/William_Bengen.

12 Rex Voegtlin and Wade D. Pfau, "Mitigating the Four Major Risks of Sustainable Inflation-Adjusted Retirement Income," white paper, Annexus Research Institute, 2014, https://www.immediateannuities.com/pdfs/articles/mitigating-the-four-major-risks-of-sustainable-inflation-adjusted-retirement-income.pdf.

change throughout retirement. "Rigid rules" and "comfortable retirement" rarely go hand in hand.

- *It uses historical market returns.*

  Analysis by Charles Schwab Investment Advisory projects that market returns for stocks and bonds over the next decade are likely to be below long-term historical averages.[13] If that prediction turns out to be true, then using higher historical market returns to calculate a sustainable withdrawal rate could result in a withdrawal rate that is too high. While you are confidently sailing along, withdrawing 4 percent plus inflation each year and assuming your money will last as long as you do, your portfolio is actually shrinking.

- *It assumes that 4 percent is enough to live on.*

  Most retirees don't look at their withdrawals on a percentage-of-portfolio basis. They look at them on a cash-flow-needed basis. If you need $60,000 a year from your portfolio, then taking just 4 percent from your $1 million savings isn't going to cover it. If your goal is simply to make your money last, then taking 1 percent or 2 percent would assure that goal. But if your goal is to live a secure, productive retirement life, then relying on a rigid distribution rule isn't going to work.

Don't invest just because something works for somebody else. You need to think about what you need yourself. We talked about the 4 percent strategy, where advisors say you will never run out of money if you stick to 4 percent withdrawals each year. That works well

---

13   Eva A. Xu and Seth McMoore, "Schwab's 2023 Long-Term Capital Market Expectations," Charles Schwab, January 3, 2023, https://www.schwab.com/learn/story/schwabs-long-term-capital-market-expectations.

for many people, but it leaves many others high and dry. In this case, while the average investor does fine, some don't. Why take the chance?

QUICK TAKES

Investment advice aimed at providing a secure retirement is everywhere, from billboards to TV infomercials to financial services blogs to your uncle George.[14] Much of it has at least a kernel of truth, but much of it is also simply rules and myths that have been passed on from advisor to advisor without anyone stopping and saying, "Wait, does this really work? Is this strategy really doing what everyone thinks it is doing?"

- **Retirement Goal:** Assure your money lasts as long as you do.

- **Roadblock:** Much of the common wisdom flowing through the investment community is actually harmful to financially conservative retirees looking for cash flow to cover bills and growth to cover inflation.

- **Solution:** Take advice with a grain of salt. Ask the advisor to walk you through facts and figures based on *your* situation and goals. How much cash flow do you need each month, and how exactly does a particular strategy get you there?

---

14   In chapter 8, I'll cover questions to ask an investment advisor.

There are three kinds of lies: lies, damned lies, and statistics.

—ATTRIBUTED TO MARK TWAIN

CHAPTER 3

DON'T TRUST AVERAGES

Calling averages "lies" is probably going too far. But they are undoubtedly one of the most misused statistics in the world of financial investment. Let's look at why.

Timing Is Everything

When choosing an investment, most people look at historical returns and choose the funds that have the highest average return over time. It seems like a no-brainer, right? Why would anyone choose a fund with a lower return? Well, it's not that easy. Two investment funds can both have a three-year 10 percent average return, yet investors in Fund A could have significantly different amounts of capital in their portfolios at the end of the three years than investors in Fund B. Sounds crazy, but it's true.

$100,000 Invested in Two Different Funds

	Fund A	Fund B
Year 1 Return	30 percent	10 percent
Year 2 Return	(10 percent)	10 percent
Year 3 Return	10 percent	10 percent
3-Year average return percent	10 percent	10 percent
	Fund A	**Fund B**
3-year result in dollars	$128,700	$133,100

Both of these investments would be shown as having a three-year average performance of 10 percent. But which would you rather have?

Figures quoted are hypothetical and for illustrative purposes only and are not necessarily indicative of past or future results of any specific investment.

Let's look at an example to see how that works.

Say that you have $100,000 to invest. Fund A goes up 30 percent in the first year, down 10 percent the second year, and then right back up 10 percent in year three. That will be reported as a 10 percent three-year average annual return.

Fund B goes up a steady 10 percent each year. That will also be shown as a three-year average annual return of 10 percent.

At the end of three years, investors in Fund A would have $128,700 in their portfolio while those in Fund B finished the third year with $133,100. How did that happen when both funds had a three-year average annual return?

$100,000 Invested in Two Different Funds

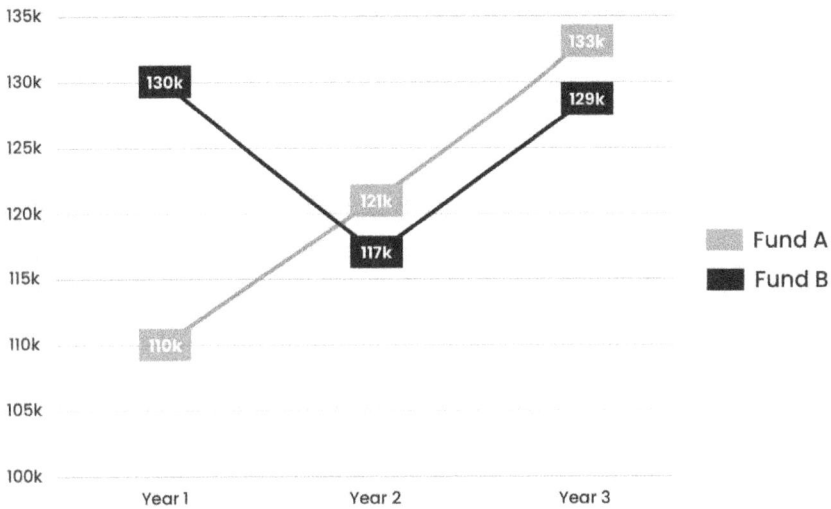

This example shows why investors need to dive into the numbers behind the averages and let the math tell the story. It's a mathematical fact that losses hurt more than gains help. When Fund A lost that 10 percent in the second year, it needed to earn more than 10 percent just to break even. That didn't happen. So, even though Fund A had the same three-year average annual return as Fund B, investors in Fund B had a larger gain overall.

To take the importance of looking behind the numbers one step further, the timing of gains and losses can actually cause a fund with a lower average annual return to outperform one with a higher average return.

Don't believe me? Let's look at the numbers again. And feel free to run the numbers yourself—the math doesn't lie, even though it can be hard to believe.

In this hypothetical example, five investors each put $10,000 per year into different funds. At the end of three years, the average annual returns ranged from 5 percent to 20 percent. If you invested based simply on the averages, it would be logical to choose the fund with the 20 percent three-year annual average. However, you would be choosing the wrong fund. The fund that actually performed better than the others over that period had a 12 percent three-year average annual return. In fact, investors in the fund with a 5 percent three-year average return fared better than those in the 20 percent fund.

Future portfolio values based on saving $10,000 a year for three years

	Fund A	Fund B	Fund C	Fund D	Fund E
3-Yr Avg Return	12%	12%	12%	5%	20%
Year 1 Return	12%	(12%)	24%	(35%)	45%
Year 2 Return	12%	24%	24%	25%	45%
Year 3 Return	12%	24%	(12%)	25%	(30%)
Ending Value	**$37,793**	**$41,307**	**$33,243**	**$38,281**	**$31,868**

Annual portfolio values based on percentage returns above

	Fund A	Fund B	Fund C	Fund D	Fund E
3-Yr Avg Return	12%	12%	12%	5%	20%
Year 1 Return	$11,200	$8,800	$12,400	$6,500	$14,500
Year 2 Return	$23,456	$23,312	$27,776	$20,625	$35,525
Year 3 Return	$37,471	$41,307	$33,243	$38,281	$31,868

How did that happen? As we noted earlier, losses hurt more than gains help. In addition, *when* those losses occur can have an outsized impact on the portfolio. As you can see in the charts above, Fund D, which ended up with a 5 percent three-year average annual return, had a large loss in the first year but then had large gains afterward. Conversely, Fund E, with the 20 percent three-year average annual return, had two really great years but then lost nearly a third of its value in the last year. Despite the early loss and its low annual average, investors in Fund D earned about 20 percent more in the three-year period than the high-average-return Fund E. An early loss can sometimes be made up; a later loss cannot.

Funds B and C are even better examples of this phenomenon. Both had a 12 percent three-year average annual return, and both had similar gains and losses, yet Fund B investors ended the three years with $37,471 in their portfolios while those in Fund C had $33,243. The difference was *when* the 12 percent loss occurred. Fund B experienced its loss in the first year while Fund C lost 12 percent in the final year. Fund B had time to make up for the loss while Fund C did not.

This annual return characteristic, where timing of losses and gains impacts the final outcome despite the overall average, is called "sequence of returns," and it is a metric that is often overlooked in favor of looking at simplified averages. As the name implies, the order of gains and losses has a significant impact on the final result. This impact is further amplified in retirement, when most people need to withdraw capital or liquidate assets monthly or annually, whether the market is up or down.

Let's look at one more example of how timing is everything. In this case, it wasn't one down year out of three that hurt returns. It was a down decade, which can happen at any time. In this example, both Paul and Bill started their retirement with $1 million in their portfolio, and both needed to earn or withdraw $50,000 each year to cover annual expenses. Paul's retirement coincided with the roaring 1990s, and ten years later, he was living his best life. Unfortunately, Bill's retirement coincided with the early 2000s and a three-year bear market.

PAUL- RETIRED IN 1990 WITH $1M
Invested in the S&P 500

YEAR	RETURN	WD	WD%	BALANCE
1990	-6.56%	$50k	5.00%	$887,680
1991	26.31%	$50k	5.63%	$1,058,074
1992	4.46%	$50k	4.73%	$1,053,034
1993	7.06%	$50k	4.75%	$1,073,848
1994	-1.54%	$50k	4.66%	$1,008,081
1995	34.11%	$50k	4.96%	$1,284,882
1996	20.26%	$50k	3.89%	$1,485,069
1997	31.01%	$50k	3.37%	$1,880,084
1998	26.67%	$50k	2.66%	$2,318,167
1999	19.53%	$50k	2.16%	$2,711,140

Average withdrawal rate: **4.18%**

BILL - RETIRED IN 2000 WITH $1M
Invested in the S&P 500

YEAR	RETURN	WD	WD%	BALANCE
2000	-10.14%	$50k	5.00%	$853,670
2001	-13.04%	$50k	5.86%	$698,871
2002	-23.37%	$50k	7.15%	$497,230
2003	26.38%	$50k	10.06%	$ 565,209
2004	8.99%	$50k	8.85%	$561,527
2005	3.00%	$50k	8.90%	$526,873
2006	13.62%	$50k	9.49%	$541,823
2007	3.53%	$50k	9.23%	$509,184
2008	-38.49%	$50k	9.82%	$282,444
2009	23.45%	$50k	17.70%	$286,952

Average withdrawal rate: **9.21%**

What a difference a few bad years made! As noted, both men started their retirement with $1 million and a $50,000 or 5 percent withdrawal rate. Yet ten years later, Paul's portfolio had grown to more than $2.7 million while Bill was looking at a slim $287,000 to fund the rest of his years.

Bill might have started his retirement withdrawing a conservative 5 percent of his portfolio, but because he had to sell into a trough during the first three years, he had to sell more shares each year to realize his required $50,000 income. If Bill had 100,000 shares of stock each worth $10 at the beginning and sold 5 percent or 5,000 shares the first year for $50,000, he now had 95,000 shares left. If the market went down and he had to sell his shares the next year at $7.50 per share, he would need to sell 6,667 shares (7 percent of his portfolio) to get his $50,000.

He now only has 88,333 shares left for a portfolio size of $662,498. What happens if the market keeps falling for another year and he now has to sell 10,000 shares at $5 each to achieve his $50,000 annual cash flow? He ends up with just 78,333 shares worth $391,665. Even if the market makes a dramatic U-turn over the next few years, Bill now only has 78,333 shares of stocks rather than 100,000.

This is a simplified example, but you can see from the chart how it could have played out given actual annual returns for the 2000s. Because the number of shares dwindled in the first three years, his withdrawal percentage crept up so that even in good years he was liquidating a significant percentage of his portfolio—more than 17 percent in the last year!

Retirement Flips the Equation

The total return equation—Growth + Income = Total Returns, or G + I = TR—is the foundation of developing an investment strategy. By the time retirement comes into play, most people have been on the growth side of the fence for forty years. But now it's time to move to the income side and learn new tricks. All the investment skills and knowledge you've learned over the years need to be thrown out the window, because your goals are now very different. Now you're taking money out, not putting money in. You're looking for monthly income, not long-term growth.

Growth + Income = Total Returns

$$G + I = TR$$

During the working years—i.e., the "accumulation phase" of your investment plan—most people focus on growth:

- The investor is putting capital into an account.

- Their employer is often contributing. Interest is compounding.

- Dividends are being reinvested.

- The stock market is going up over the decades.

It's grow, grow, grow. And if there are a few downturns along the way, it simply means they can buy shares at a lower price and get a good deal. In this phase, we put the G in the total return equation front and center.

When it comes time to retire, however, we need to flip the equation. We are no longer putting savings into a fund. We don't have an employer to contribute. Instead of compounding and being reinvested, withdrawals are being made, and dividends are being spent. However, in retirement the focus should not be on growth but on income, with income being the money that has accumulated from your investments. Income is the name of the game in retirement.

I had a person in my office recently who was raving about the mutual fund he had been in for decades. I agreed that he had made a lot of money, but he could have made more if he had dug below the averages. Over time, the majority of mutual funds fall below the S&P average.

However, he had a nice portfolio as he was going into retirement and thought he'd just stay with the mutual fund. This fund has more than $100 billion in assets, so he obviously isn't alone. I didn't want to tell him he was wrong—no one wants to hear that—so I simply showed him the numbers behind the fund's growth and let him draw his own conclusions. This particular fund, as well as many in the same class, got almost 100 percent of its total return from growth. Only 0.46 percent of the total came from income.

Why is that important to know? In the distribution phase of life, retirees need to realize income from their investments to cover everyday expenses. They can get that income by selling shares of funds in their portfolio (though we've seen how that can backfire in the earlier charts), or they can get it directly from the yields on the shares they own. Relying on growth means relying on the market trending upward year after year, month after month. Covering expenses via an investment yield component provides a more consistent, stable income that protects your principal.

Withdrawing cash from your portfolio adds a new factor to the equation, one that has a huge impact on the total return. Let's look at two charts to see just how much a portfolio can be hurt if the withdrawals are not covered by the income value of the equation. The first chart illustrates the growth over time when the investor is able to let their money ride. The other shows what happens to the same portfolio when the retiree needs to withdraw $50,000 per year.

Worker with $1 million portfolio in 2000 who can let their money ride

Year	S&P Annual Return	Annual Deposit/ Withdrawal	Management Fee	Cumulative Fees	Beginning of Year Value	End of Year Value
2000	-9.10 %	$ 0	$9,678.48	$9,678.48	$1,000,000	$899,938
2001	-11.89 %	$ 0	$8,100.05	$17,778.53	$899,938	$785,038.31
2002	-22.10 %	$ 0	$6,783.11	$24,561.65	$785,038.31	$605,476.48
2003	28.67 %	$ 0	$6,696.14	$31,257.79	$605,476.48	$771,282.66
2004	10.88 %	$ 0	$7,900.46	$39,158.25	$771,282.66	$846,652.27
2005	4.91 %	$ 0	$8,481.24	$47,639.50	$846,652.27	$879,355.61
2006	15.78 %	$ 0	$9,338.24	$56,977.74	$879,355.61	$1,007,954.58
2007	5.57 %	$ 0	$10,561.25	$67,538.99	$1,007,954.58	$1,053,518.78
2008	-37.00 %	$ 0	$8,776.46	$76,315.45	$1,053,518.78	$657,111.35
2009	26.45 %	$ 0	$6,967.61	$83,283.06	$657,111.35	$822,634.04
2010	15.06 %	$ 0	$8,392.35	$91,675.41	$822,634.04	$937,089.73
2011	2.11 %	$ 0	$9,600.35	$101,275.76	$937,089.73	$947,296.03
2012	15.99 %	$ 0	$10,519.03	$111,794.79	$947,296.03	$1,087,829.85
2013	32.37 %	$ 0	$12,690.83	$124,485.62	$1,087,829.85	$1,425,635.52
2014	13.67 %	$ 0	$15,093.39	$139,579.01	$1,425,635.52	$1,604,449.35
2015	1.37 %	$ 0	$16,092.82	$155,671.82	$1,604,449.35	$1,610,255.29
2016	11.95 %	$ 0	$16,712.47	$172,384.30	$1,610,255.29	$1,784,699.99
2017	21.82 %	$ 0	$19,776.29	$192,160.59	$1,784,699.99	$2,152,454.52
2018	-4.30 %	$ 0	$22,171.05	$214,331.64	$2,152,454.52	$2,037,376.60
2019	31.47 %	$ 0	$24,029.95	$238,361.59	$2,037,376.60	$2,651,963.88
2020	18.39 %	$ 0	$26,558.40	$264,919.99	$2,651,963.88	$3,108,322.12
2021	28.68 %	$ 0	$35,519.97	$300,439.96	$3,108,322.12	$3,959,934.27
2022	-18.13 %	$ 0	$34,003.05	$334,443.01	$3,959,934.27	$3,209,848.33

The twenty-year average annual S&P return is the same for both investors—6.05 percent over those two decades. But as you can see, the results are very different. Instead of ending up with a portfolio worth $3.2 million, the retiree has run out of money.

Whoa! How did that happen? It happened because adding withdrawals to the equation changes the outcome. The retiree was taking $50,000 out each year (most retirees take out what they need, not a set percentage) whether the market was up or down. Although it

Retiree with $1 million portfolio in 2000 who needs $50,000 per year from their portfolio

Year	S&P Annual Return	Annual Deposit/ Withdrawal	Management Fee	Cumulative Fees	Beginning of Year Value	End of Year Value
2000	-9.10%	$ -50000	$9,411.07	$9,411.07	$1,000,000	$853,362.85
2001	-11.89%	$ -50000	$7,424.24	$16,835.31	$853,362.85	$695,696.11
2002	-22.10%	$ -50000	$5,764.85	$22,600.16	$695,696.11	$491,417.55
2003	28.67%	$ -50000	$5,136.77	$27,736.93	$491,417.55	$567,932.58
2004	10.88%	$ -50000	$5,542.52	$33,279.45	$567,932.58	$569,807.94
2005	4.91%	$ -50000	$5,431.05	$38,710.50	$569,807.94	$539,943.87
2006	15.78%	$ -50000	$5,453.05	$44,163.55	$539,943.87	$564,851.31
2007	5.57%	$ -50000	$5,642.12	$49,805.66	$564,851.31	$540,463.83
2008	-37.00%	$ -50000	$4,264.97	$54,070.63	$540,463.83	$298,739.01
2009	26.45%	$ -50000	$2,856.01	$56,926.65	$298,739.01	$313,931.75
2010	15.06%	$ -50000	$2,922.55	$59,849.20	$313,931.75	$301,593.16
2011	2.11%	$ -50000	$2,825.99	$62,675.19	$301,593.16	$255,430.39
2012	15.99%	$ -50000	$2,558.55	$65,233.73	$255,430.39	$241,563.79
2013	32.37%	$ -50000	$2,527.90	$67,761.63	$241,563.79	$260,166.46
2014	13.67%	$ -50000	$2,470.37	$70,232	$260,166.46	$239,537.54
2015	1.37%	$ -50000	$2,132	$72,364	$239,537.54	$190,335.59
2016	11.95%	$ -50000	$1,691.44	$74,055.44	$190,335.59	$157,440.86
2017	21.82%	$ -50000	$1,459.28	$75,514.72	$157,440.86	$135,331.28
2018	-4.39%	$ -50000	$1,122.79	$76,637.50	$135,331.28	$82,074.62
2019	31.47%	$ -50000	$682.54	$77,320.04	$82,074.62	$51,498.36
2020	18.39%	$ -50000	$219.48	$77,539.52	$51,498.36	$1,248.13
2021	28.68%	$ -50000	-$278.49	$77,261.02	$1,248.13	-$54,463.27
2022	-18.13%	$ -50000	-$725.32	$76,535.70	-$54,463.27	-$91,558.79

averaged 6.05 percent, there were several years when it was in negative territory—yet the investor still needed to pull out that $50,000. In those down years, they were selling into the trough whether they wanted to or not. They needed the income, so they had to.

By the time I finished showing my new client these charts, he was beginning to think maybe staying in his mutual growth fund with a double-digit annual return wasn't such a good idea.

But I wasn't finished.

I dug even deeper into the numbers as we looked at the downside of relying on annual average returns.

Retirees usually need income every month. Many retirees look at their fund statement at the end of the year and see that it had a 15 percent return. That's pretty good, right? However, that same retiree looks at their portfolio balance and sees they now have less in it than they did at this time last year. What happened? How did the fund go up by more than they were withdrawing but their portfolio balance went down?

A second look shows that in addition to some really good months, the fund had several down months. Imagine a jagged sawtooth—up some months, down others. Maybe in the up months the retiree was able to sell 333 shares at $15 per share to get the $5,000 needed each month. Keeping things simple, let's say the retiree started with 10,000 shares and now has 9,667 shares. Next month, the market falls, and they need to sell 500 shares at $10 per share to achieve the same $5,000. Now the retiree has 9,167 shares. Oh no, it falls another month, and they need to sell 1,000 shares at $5 per share. Now, even if the market goes back up, the retiree is only going to realize the gain on 8,167 shares rather than the original 10,000. And even if the market gains mean that the portfolio value increases, the retiree is likely still going to be selling shares each month. Each month, there are fewer shares in the portfolio to take advantage of the market upswing, and every hiccup is magnified.

Selling fund shares each month to cover cash flow might work for a while. Maybe even for a few years. But the ups and downs of the market will eventually catch up with you. Selling shares is simply not a sustainable strategy.

Retirement Is All about Income

My new client had seen the light and was ready to make some changes. Now he was asking exactly what changes I would suggest. This is where a specialist in income investing comes into play. Nearly all advisors can provide their clients with adequate strategies for growing a portfolio.

G = Growth/Loss (Capital Appreciation)*
I = Interest/Dividends
TR = Total Return

*Historically, total return has averaged 10-11 percent; 6-7 percent came from growth and 2-3 percent came from interest and dividends.

What they often can't do is change the strategy to provide a conservative plan, based on individual stocks and bonds, for generating enough income to cover current cash flow needs and preserving principal while also allowing for moderate growth. I like to view it as flipping the equation from the traditional G + I = TR to I + G = TR.

**Investment Formula
During Working Years**

$$G + I = TR$$

**Income Formula
During Retirement**

$$I + G = TR$$

The focus is now on income. We still consider growth, but it is secondary. We need to align the portfolio with the retiree's new purpose and goals, and that means focusing on income.

It means focusing on what works for your specific purpose and looking below the averages to find the right strategy.

One of the primary reasons I am so focused on income is that I know how important it is to protect the principal. If the principal is reduced, the income will follow. In the next chapter, I'll outline some things you can do to protect that all-important principal and help ensure it will last as long as you do.

QUICK TAKES

Averages can be relevant when comparing similar investments in the same economic period—you don't want to invest in a fund that *consistently* underperformed. But averages can be misleading. It's important to dig down and see exactly *how* those averages were achieved.

- **Retirement Goal:** Generate enough income to cover daily expenses.

- **Roadblock:** Average annual returns are often made up primarily of the growth component, making it hard to determine which investments are best for income. In addition, they don't take into account management fees, inflation, and monthly withdrawals.

- **Solution:** Don't be fooled by data relying on annual return averages. Dig down and run scenarios that fit your specific goals to find the mixture of stocks and bonds that consistently provide the income you need with a minimum amount of asset liquidation.

The individual investor should
act consistently as an investor
and not as a speculator.

–BEN GRAHAM

CHAPTER 4

RISK MANAGEMENT—
PROTECT YOUR ASSETS!

You may not know this, but three of the largest farming operations in the United States are not corporations but family owned.[15]

Here they are:[16]

LARSEN FARMS

87,104 acres—potatoes, alfalfa

Blaine Larsen started Larsen Farms with an initial purchase of eighty acres of sagebrush-covered land near Hamer, Idaho, that cost him $2,400, or $30 an acre. Today, Larsen Farms grosses more than $400 million annually.

GAYLON LAWRENCE JR.

115,000 acres—citrus, corn, cotton, rice, soybeans, wine grapes, winter wheat

---

15　Successful Farming Staff, "3 of the biggest US farmers," Successful Farming, July 21, 2022, https://www.agriculture.com/farm-management/farm-land/3-of-the-biggest-us-farmers.

16　Ibid.

Gaylon Lawrence Jr. oversees The Lawrence Group, a diverse portfolio of companies. The group's agribusiness manages more than 115,000 acres from coast to coast, including 42,000 acres of farmland on the Arkansas side of the Mississippi River.

SCULLY FAMILY

106,725 acres–tenant farming

William Scully founded this enterprise in the mid-nineteenth century. He leased his lands to tenant farmers and grew his portfolio to more than 225,000 acres. Today, his heirs oversee more than 100,000 acres of those original holdings.

As you can imagine, each of these farming operations has gone through years of plenty and years of drought. However, each family has focused on protecting their farm's assets—the land itself. Think about this: If, during drought years, the families had sold their land to gain capital, their farming operations would be a fraction of their acreage today. However, each family realized that without retaining land—and buying more whenever possible—their yearly income would actually decrease over the long run.

Just like these family farming operations, it is imperative that you protect your assets! And if you invest the right way, the income produced by your assets will sustain you throughout your retirement years.

People are very bad at assessing risk. How many of us will drive hundreds of miles because we feel safer driving than flying? How many people tremble at the idea of sharks yet step into a bathtub or shower every day? We are many times more likely to be injured in a car crash than in a plane crash. Even more likely are we to be injured in a fall than we are to be eaten by sharks.

While putting more emphasis on avoiding sharks than bathtubs isn't going to make a major difference in how most people live, putting too much emphasis on the wrong risks to your investment portfolio can result in a retirement focused on counting pennies instead of enjoying life. When you are working and in the accumulation phase, you can afford to take some risk because you have time to make up losses. When you are retired, losses to your principal can be permanent. Protecting the principal should become a primary goal. Most retirees understand this. Yet a fair number protect against things that are unlikely to affect their portfolio while ignoring things that are. Even those who recognize the true risks often fail to adequately protect their principal.

■　■　■

I had a couple come in to see me a few months ago. Let's call them Tom and Mary. Tom was an accountant, and Mary was a special education teacher. They had not yet applied for Social Security, but they had two pensions between them that totaled $100,000 per year. In addition, Tom had an $850,000 IRA and Mary had her own retirement fund worth $750,000. Tom was taking $24,000 out of his IRA each year, and Mary was taking about $14,000 from hers. Although their $1.6 million combined retirement portfolios were only generating about 1 percent in income, it seemed they were doing fine, especially knowing that they would eventually add income from Social Security.

While going over their assets together, I was wondering why they were in my office. Most people come because they need more income to live on. That did not seem to be this couple.

It took a little more discussion, but I soon realized that what they really wanted was advice on how to reduce investment risk. Mary had already committed $90,000 to an annuity to try to balance the risk in the remaining stock-heavy, growth-focused portfolio. She was aiming for a combined 5 percent return. Tom was even more risk averse. He had about half his money in a risk-free annuity, with the other half in stocks. But he was hoping for an even greater return—8 percent—on the combined annuity and stock portfolio.

This is where two realities crashed into each other like a head-on collision on the highway.

Tom can get an 8 percent return, but he isn't going to achieve it with the conservative, low-risk profile he wanted. A conservative investment cannot make 8 percent no matter what you do. And he certainly wasn't going to get a combined 8 percent when half the portfolio is capped at 1 percent. To get that combined total, the other half of the portfolio is going to have to average 15 percent. That means Tom is going to have to get some growth, which introduces risk. The more growth he needs, the more risk he takes on.

Now that I knew about the annuity, it changed the entire conversation. Tom wasn't taking $24,000 out of an $850,000 portfolio. He was taking $24,000 per year out of a $425,000 portfolio, with the rest tied up in the annuity. That means he is removing more than 5 percent from his stocks and bonds portfolio each year. We've already noted that this portfolio is generating only 1 percent in income, so what do you think is happening to the principal? That's right—it is slowly being reduced, because the growth portion of the portfolio isn't covering the income needed.

This is where we circle back to the premise that people are horrible at assessing risk. Both Tom and Mary thought they were reducing the risk in their portfolio because they had invested heavily in "safe" annuities that would provide guaranteed income. *In reality, they were increasing the risk to their assets!*

By placing a significant portion of their investment portfolio into an annuity that provided only a 1 percent income return, they were both increasing the risk they were going to need to take in their IRAs if they were going to hit their investment goals of 5 percent and 8 percent.

So, what are Tom and Mary to do?

- They could reduce their living expenses and the amount of capital they are withdrawing from their portfolio.

- They could take on more risk to try to boost their growth stocks.

- They could continue as they are and cross their fingers that everything turns out all right.

- They could adjust their portfolio to increase income while reducing true risk.

What looks like the most attractive option to you?

Income to the Rescue

Many people don't consider income as part of the investment return, but it is really the foundation. If you have intentionally and proactively (and reliably!) maximized your income stream, everything else will follow. Let me explain.

Let's pretend that Tom put half his portfolio into an annuity with a 1 percent income cap. That means having his entire $850,000 portfolio to work with in the quest for a safe 8 percent return. As mentioned earlier, only 1 percent of the returns are currently from income. That means he is relying on 7 percent from his growth stocks to provide the return he needs.

While income is consistent, growth is a wild card. You can't count on it. You can guess based on past performance, but you can't know for sure that a specific stock or fund will grow 7 percent each year. In fact, you can be pretty sure it won't. The average S&P growth over decades has been around 6 percent—sometimes much more, sometimes much less—on an annual basis. But overall, it is unlikely that an investor is going to consistently achieve a 7 percent growth rate year in and year out. Many retirees would need to achieve that growth month in and month out, because they need the income on a monthly basis.

That type of consistency is even less likely to occur than a 7 percent annual return. And retirees need consistency, because they are using their portfolios to fund their current lifestyle. They are no longer saving for the future. However, if you are able to achieve a 5 percent income return via dividends and interest, which is very doable, you only need to find 3 percent via growth. That is a very different risk story than if you are looking for consistent 7 percent growth to boost a 1 percent income return.

But income doesn't just anchor a portfolio. It can also be used to supercharge a portfolio. Let's look at how that works.

For the twenty-year period covering 2000 to 2020, the S&P averaged a little over 6 percent per year. One-third of that return came from the dividends.[17] So, that's 4 percent growth and 2 percent income. If you started with $1 million in 2000 and it grew at 4 percent a year—the two-thirds of the 6 percent that the S&P rose—you would end up with a little over $2.1 million at the end of 2019.

---

17   "Stock Market Returns between 2000 and 2020," Official Data, accessed May 7, 2024, https://www.officialdata.org/us/stocks/s-p-500/2000?amount=100&endYear=2020.

Add in the 2 percent income component, and you end up with more than $3.1 million. That looks pretty good … but you can do better.

Instead of just riding the wave of the average S&P growth, imagine that you construct your portfolio to optimize the income. On that original $1 million, you could earn about 4 percent in dividends using individual stocks that could potentially add another 4 percent in growth during the same period. Add that 4 percent income to the 4 percent growth rate the S&P averaged, and you have an 8 percent rate of return. So, what does that do to your portfolio? You are now looking at a $4.5 million bucket to use to support your retirement. That's a full million more, because you were intentional in setting up an income-driven portfolio.

People want to maximize what they have, and they can do that by maximizing income. Tom was only making 1 percent in income on his portfolio. If he is taking out $24,000, he is eating into principal. If, however, he invests in highly rated income stocks and specific bonds instead of his current growth-oriented stocks, he can easily get up to $20,000 in income on his $425,000 portfolio. That means he just needs $4,000 per year in growth. That can be done consistently by taking less risk and without impacting his principal.

Tom and Mary probably don't need the extra income that can be achieved by intentionally setting up an income-driven portfolio. Between their pensions, Social Security, and a small income from their current portfolio, they will likely be able to cover their expenses. But even if someone is doing well, like this couple, they would always like to be doing better. It isn't always about living expenses. Who wouldn't want more money to give to a favorite charity or leave to the children and grandchildren? I had a client who loved our income message. It was important for him to be able to give to his church. When we were able to restructure his portfolio to get more income, he felt that he could give more because he had "found" money. That was important to him, and it made his life more meaningful.

The Unseen Risk

Tom and Mary were correct that reducing risk and protecting their assets was important. As noted in an earlier chapter, retirees often fail to make the switch from focusing on growth to focusing on income in retirement. However, the mistake they made is the same one many retirees make: they confused a "stable" investment with a "safe" investment. Certain fixed annuities and Treasury bills are stable. The principal is going to remain the same throughout the life of the investment, and it is going to pay a predetermined income stream, but both products involve too-often-ignored risks that can negatively affect a retiree's assets.

When retirees talk about avoiding risk, they tend to focus on losing money in a stock market crash. Most have lived through several major financial crashes that lasted years, and they want to avoid the consequences of another downturn in retirement. They talk to their financial advisor, who tells them the safest investments are Treasuries—which are government backed—and annuities, which guarantee an income. Treasury bills protect the principal from market declines, as do many annuities. These investments are indeed safe, if all you want is for the principal to remain intact. They aren't going to crash, based on claims being paid by a particular insurance company.

But fixed income investments, such as Treasuries and annuities, have hidden risks—or at least risks that aren't often considered. Three or five or ten years from now, the retiree can get back the principal they put into a T-bill and, depending on the contract, can often get back the principal invested in an annuity. *However, during the length of investment, the retiree is going to lose the ability to make money with their money.*

They'll lose buying power because these investments rarely keep up with inflation. They lose the flexibility to adjust their portfolio if the investment climate or their own needs change. Annuities and T-bills lock in the investment. Penalties can be steep for those who want to exit early. And the interest they receive is usually less than they could achieve with safe, income-producing stocks. All these factors put stress on the principal, which remains stagnant.

Neither Treasuries nor annuities are inherently poor choices for retirees. In fact, given the right circumstances, they can be an important part of an income-focused portfolio. But let's look at a few of the things that advisors and insurance salespeople often fail to point out when pitching them to their clients.

Getting What You Pay For

US Treasuries, such as Treasury bills, notes, and bonds, are a favorite fixed income vehicle for retirees. Treasury bills are backed by the full faith and credit of the US government. If held to maturity, T-bills are considered virtually risk-free. Investors are guaranteed to get their principal back plus whatever interest rate they accepted at time of purchase. However, there are several reasons why someone might choose not to invest in these vehicles:

- *Low Returns*

    Although US Treasuries are touted as one of the safest investments available, that safety comes at the expense of yields. These bonds are often called "cash equivalents" because they are nearly as safe as cash, but the yield is typically much lower than other investment options.

- *Inflation Risk*
  While Treasuries are considered safe, they may not keep pace with inflation, which can erode the purchasing power of your investment over time. If inflation rates exceed the yield on your Treasury investment, you could effectively be losing money in real terms.

- *Opportunity Cost*
  Investing in Treasuries ties up your capital, potentially preventing you from taking advantage of other investment opportunities with higher returns.

- *Interest Rate Risk*
  When interest rates rise, the market value of existing Treasuries tends to decrease. If you need to sell your Treasury securities before maturity, you might receive less than your initial investment.

- *Early-Withdrawal Penalties*
  If you need to sell Treasury bonds or notes before their maturity date, you may incur penalties or receive a lower price than their face value, potentially leading to a loss.

- *Need to Roll Over at Current Rates*
  T-bills can make sense in high-rate environments, but what happens in a few years when the bills mature? The retiree will need to renew the bill at what is often a much lower rate. This means that monthly income will also fall.

Looking more closely at annuities, we see they often carry the same risks as Treasuries, plus a few of their own.

Unlike a Treasury bill, which is set up like a bond, an annuity is a contract between an insurance company and the purchaser. The purchaser gives the insurance company a pool of capital, and the insurance company provides monthly payments to the retiree. Annuities come in a variety of forms, but each contract will specify when payments begin, the duration of payments, the interest rate paid on the capital covered by the contract, whether interest is fixed or adjusted, what happens to the initial capital at the end of the contract, and other details of how the annuity owner receives their monthly income payments.

The contracts can be complicated, but annuities have one thing in common. They are underwritten and sold by insurance companies. And insurance companies are not in the business of losing money. Although the contract usually guarantees a minimum interest rate, depending on claims being paid, you can be sure the insurance company is achieving a higher interest rate with your money.

In addition, annuities are only backed by the insurance company. All this means that although annuities are considered safe, they are only as safe as the company that backs them.

That brings us to the primary annuity misconception. Annuities are often sold as investments. Annuities are not investments. They provide longevity insurance. They are designed to provide income for a set period of time, sometimes for life. They guarantee you will never run out of income. *But they don't guarantee that income will be enough to live on.*

When you buy an annuity, all you've done is eliminate the downside. You've protected or insured your principal. The question is this: Are you still going to be able to generate the return you need to be able to get you through retirement and increasing inflation?

Annuities have become extremely popular because guaranteed income always sounds attractive. Who doesn't want guaranteed mailbox money? Plus, these agents make a significant commission when they sell an annuity; any money that is put into an annuity does not have fiduciary oversight, making it a commissionable product. Therefore, they emphasize the positive and skim over the negative. The agents like to focus on recent history and best-case scenarios. They promise a return based on cherry-picked years. Retirees often walk away believing an annuity provides a guaranteed high return with no risk. That can't be done, so don't believe the hype.

When a client brings an annuity proposal to us to look at, we tell them to look at the entire presentation. The proposal will usually show different payouts based on no return, moderate return, and aggressive return. It will also outline a best-case scenario, an average scenario, and a worst-case scenario. The worst-case scenario is usually buried somewhere toward the end, as are the fees that eat into returns. We tell people to look at the worst-case scenario, circle it, highlight it. We also tell people to buy an annuity for what it *will* do, not for what you *think* it will do.

A Better Way to Protect Assets

People hear the word *stocks*, and they think *risky*. They hear the word *annuity*, and they think *safe*. But as I've noted, Treasury bills and annuities can provide a stable income, but they don't necessarily protect a retiree's assets. If inflation is higher than the annuity or Treasury return—and it usually is—the retiree will be losing buying power and likely dipping into their assets to cover the gap.

While annuities and Treasuries aren't the perfect answer, retirees do need to be careful when it comes to stocks. They aren't wrong when they have the impression that stocks are risky. Advisors will also often push mutual funds because they are professionally managed and spread risk across many different equities. However, these funds are usually so big that they simply track the S&P while charging high fees. To protect their assets, retirees need to find ways to use stocks that don't fall as far as the average equity.

Stocks are definitely more volatile than Treasury bills or annuities. But a $1 million portfolio invested in dividend, income-focused stocks can consistently generate $40,000 to $45,000 each year in dividends while positioning the portfolio for potential growth to keep up with inflation. This is a significantly better return than you typically get with T-bills or annuities, plus the portfolio is able to keep up and often beat inflation.

I can hear you saying, "But what if the market goes down?"

If the market declines—and we know it will at times—these stocks continue paying dividends. They continue to pay interest. The decline in share price does not affect the income payout. The whole purpose of an income-focused portfolio is to avoid spending the principal. If you are not selling shares in a down market, the portfolio has a good chance of recovering when the market goes back up. If you can avoid selling shares of your principal in the early phase of your retirement, you will have more money available if needed when expenses, especially medical expenses, increase in your later years. You won't have to access the principal if you are still getting consistent income. To use an old analogy, during the down time, the chickens might get skinnier, but they are still laying eggs.

■ ■ ■

When Tom and Mary came to me, they actually had the right idea. As they approached retirement, they needed to protect their assets. Their problem was that they didn't understand all the risks their portfolio faced and that putting capital into the wrong income vehicle actually increased risk for the rest of their portfolio. Annuities, Treasuries bills, and other fixed income products tout themselves as safe, secure, and the perfect answer. They are not perfect, as Tom and Mary came to realize.

That doesn't mean there is no place for them. With the demise of pensions, annuities can give a bit of comfort by providing a monthly income that used to come from pensions. Retirees just need to understand what they are buying, and it isn't a one-size-fits-all situation. For example, today's high-rate environment is actually a very good time to lock in an annuity or T-bill rate. They are paying between 5.5 and 6.0 percent, with no risk to your principal. That is hard to say no to. In fact, you probably shouldn't say no. Inflation appears to have been brought under control, and rates will likely decrease in the coming years. Locking in 6 percent now is good retirement advice.

However, the trick is to make sure the annuity is fixed. You want to lock in that high interest rate for the life of the T-bill or annuity. The most popular annuity being purchased today is an adjustable-rate version. This is sold on the premise that its interest rate will increase as inflation increases, thus overcoming the risk that inflation will eat into the returns. Insurance companies like this version because it also means they can lower your interest rates if rates fall. They don't typically emphasize that part in the sales presentation. You don't want to put your capital into a product that will be paying out less interest in a year or two than it is now. Despite their downsides, annuities are not inherently dangerous to your overall assets. Just be sure to know what you are buying.

In the next chapter, I'll dive even deeper into how even well-intentioned and very common investment advice can prove hazardous to a retiree's security—and it doesn't have to be that way.

QUICK TAKES

Retirees usually set up their portfolios to avoid things like market crashes, medical costs, and rising expenses that could negatively impact their retirement. What they often don't emphasize enough is the insidious danger created by dipping into principal to pay everyday expenses.

- Income is the foundation of a sustainable portfolio.
- Stable does not equal safe.
- An income-focused portfolio of dividend-paying stocks and bonds can provide consistent income while protecting principal.

Everything old is new again.

-ATTRIBUTED TO JONATHAN SWIFT

CHAPTER 5

REVERSE INVESTING

We spend our working lives building a nest egg for the day we can retire. For years we—and often our employers—consistently add to our portfolio. Then one day we no longer have an income to cover expenses while we put money away for the future. We no longer have an employer to boost investments. The world turns upside down, and we need to reverse gears. When you're in retirement, it's not about what you are saving, investing, and reinvesting; it's about what you are taking out.

Many retirees are surprised to find out how much harder it is to manage their portfolio in retirement than it was to build wealth during their working years. They just assumed that once they had accumulated their nest egg, it would be smooth sailing and they'd never have to worry about money again. It's a rude awakening when they realize their principal is being depleted and they might have to cut back on their lifestyle.

This change in focus is a little like doing the Saturday errands. Imagine that you head out the door and get in the car. You know exactly what you need to do, and you just want to get it done quickly so you can get back home to enjoy the rest of your weekend. You head over to the hardware store to pick up some touch-up paint to refresh the front door. You do a quick stop at the gas station to fill up for the week. Then you drop off some clothes at Goodwill. Finally, you hit the grocery store and get what you'll need for a week's worth of dinners. You know your town well, and if you were able to drive in your sleep, you'd be making these stops while in dreamland. In fact, you've driven this route so often, you sometimes find yourself daydreaming instead of paying attention to the road.

Now imagine you have to drive the car in reverse. Suddenly, streets and turns you know like the back of your hand need your complete focus to navigate. You need to drive much slower and really pay attention. The route is the same. The stops are the same. But the experience is entirely different. Your goal now isn't to get done as fast as possible. It's to get it all done safely.

This is what investing in retirement is like. You have spent your life driving forward. You knew exactly what to do to grow wealth. You rarely had to think about it. Now, however, your financial life has made a one-eighty. Instead of accumulating wealth, you are spending it. You are driving in reverse and need to adjust your mindset to focus on your new goal.

This is the time of life when "reverse investing" jumps front and center. What is reverse investing? Well, it's one of those phrases that has two definitions—one good, the other not so good.

Defining Reverse Investing

We can look at reverse investing two different ways. The definition that fits the strategy of many retirees focuses on what is happening to the principal in their portfolio. However, successful accumulation strategies focused on growth don't work in retirement. In fact, they can hurt in retirement. Instead of growing a portfolio, growth strategies often leave the retiree with less than they started with. They are investing in reverse.

On the other hand, we can look at reverse investing as flipping the growth and the income components in our total return formula. For most of our lives, we focus on growth, so the formula used is $G + I = TR$ (Growth + Income = Total Returns). But in retirement, income becomes the primary goal, so we reverse the formula and focus on $I + G = TR$.

It's not easy to make this change. We talked earlier about how hard change can be. But changing to an income-focused portfolio can be even harder than changing some other investment strategies. Why? Well, frankly, it's just not as much fun. When you are building your portfolio, you often get to ride large waves up. You see the portfolio grow and hit milestones. Your competitive juices are flowing, and each win feels like a personal validation of how responsible and skilled you are. It's all very satisfying. However, moving to a dividend- and interest-based portfolio provides consistent income, but it rarely has those growth jumps that make your heart pound. It's closer to floating down a lazy river than surfing the waves.

When you watch interviews of people who have climbed Mount Everest, you will often hear them marvel at how unexpectedly easy the ascent was, while the descent was unexpectedly treacherous. They were being driven by adrenaline on the way up. As they hit each milestone or base camp, they would get an extra boost of energy. But when it came time to come down, the adrenaline was gone. They were tired after the long climb up. There was no energy boost as they hit the base camps, only relief to be safe inside a tent. It was hard to force themselves back out into the cold for the next leg down. This is a great analogy for building wealth.

Accumulating wealth is the easy part. It's fun, and you can see progress, just like going up the mountain. It's in retirement that people get in trouble, just like those coming down the mountain. According to some research, more than half the Mount Everest climber deaths have occurred during the descent.[18] Retirees don't need to be one of those statistics.

Who Should Avoid Investing in Reverse?

Some of you are probably asking if everyone needs to make these changes. Frankly, not everyone needs to invest this way, but I'd wager most will want to. However, if any of the following scenarios match your current and future needs, being aware of reverse investing will serve you well.

- *Those who need more than 1 or 2 percent from their portfolio in retirement*

  If you fall into this category, you are going to have to either sell shares or readjust your portfolio to bring in more income. Chances are you are going to need more from your portfolio than you think. Retirement, especially in the early years when you are likely to be more active than you anticipated, can be much more expensive than you thought it would be. Is this the time to cut back on the life you've earned? Not if you don't need to. And you probably won't need to if you make sure your portfolio is focused on income rather than growth.

  Most people don't think about the future and what the impact of inflation will be on their income. I had a gentleman in my

---

18   Jordan Lite, "Death on Mt. Everest: The Perils of the Descent," *Scientific American*, December 10, 2008, https://blogs.scientificamerican.com/news-blog/death-on-mount-everest-the-perils-o-2008-12-10/.

office who has been a client of mine since 2013. We had an $800-per-month buffer in his investment returns. That means he had almost $10,000 a year more than he needed. Guess what he told me? He said it's been a tough year, even though he's making all his ends meet. His wants, however, have begun to concern him. When he was working, he was only filling his "wants" time on the weekend because his other days were at work. Now he is filling all seven days with activities that cost money—and he's seeing his buffer shrinking. He is still OK, but he's concerned.

- *Those who are being forced to take required minimum distributions out of their tax-advantaged funds*
  When you turn seventy-three, you are required to take out almost 4 percent of your tax-advantaged portfolio, and that percentage increases each and every year.[19] If that 4 percent or more isn't covered by income, you will be dipping into your principal.

- *Those who want to reduce the risk while increasing their returns*
  I've never met anybody that doesn't want to do that in retirement. Everybody wants to reduce the risk and maximize their returns. And what do I mean by reducing the risk? We talked about that in the last chapter, but the best way to reduce risk is to define your end goal and then make sure your strategies line up with reaching it.

The end goal in retirement is having enough income to cover expenses and wants. The best way to achieve this is to stick

---

19   "Required Minimum Distribution Calculator," AARP, Updated April 29, 2024, https://www.aarp.org/retirement/required-minimum-distribution-calculator/.

with the fundamentals, which means having reliable true income in the form of interest and dividends. You are not creating income by selling shares each and every year and eroding principal. For that strategy to work, you have to trust the crystal ball that says the market will go up enough each year to cover the distribution. Any crystal ball that tells you that is no good and should not be trusted. The market is not going to go up every year, and you will end up depleting principal.

In my experience, nearly all retirees need their portfolio to provide more than 1 or 2 percent in income, especially because retirement is now often twenty or thirty years long. That is much too long to expect a nest egg to last if it is being nibbled at each month. In addition, most retirees will need to take required minimum distributions from their IRAs. And who doesn't want to reduce risk? All this adds up to an argument for avoiding investing in reverse.

The Dollar-Cost Averaging Dilemma

Changing direction in the middle of the stream is harder than many think. One of the primary and most trusted ways of earning wealth is dollar-cost averaging. This strategy involves investing the same amount of money in a target security at regular intervals, regardless of price. By using dollar-cost averaging, investors may lower their average cost per share and reduce the impact of volatility on their portfolios.

For example, a worker might have $100 taken out of their paycheck each pay period to buy stock for their company-sponsored 401(k) plan. Depending on the price of shares, this $100 would buy more shares in a down market and fewer shares in a rising market. In this case, it is actually helpful to buy into down or crashing markets because that same $100 can purchase more shares. Over time, the ups and downs of a long-term market typically average out. This strategy works so well when accumulating money that it is hard to believe it will fall apart in retirement. However, it can be a way to lose wealth as fast as it's accumulated.

In retirement, you don't put the same amount of money into your portfolio each month. Instead, you often take out a set amount to pay your monthly expenses. In other words, you are dollar-cost averaging in reverse. While dollar-cost averaging is an excellent way to accumulate wealth, it acts in reverse in retirement. When the market is down, it depletes the portfolio faster because you are selling more shares than when the market is up.

Let's look at how the math works to benefit accumulation during the working years but accelerates depletion during retirement.

■ ■ ■

Let's say that during your working years, you decided to put $100 from each paycheck into stock market–based funds. For the sake of simplicity, let's just say you stop after two months. The first month the price of each share was $10, and the second month it was $5 a share. So, you bought ten shares the first month, and when the stock price dropped to $5 a share, you bought twenty shares. Everyone always loves it when the market is soaring, but you actually create more wealth whenever the market drops because you can buy more shares.

What was the average share price between the $10 per share paid during the first month and the $5 per share paid during the second month? This is the type of math question you'll find in brain teaser games. At first glance, most people would say the average price per share was $7.50. But they'd be wrong. The average price is actually $6.65. To get the true average, you need to divide the total of what you spent by the number of shares you bought. You spent a total of $200, but you bought a total of thirty shares, because you were able to double the number of shares purchased when the price fell. Dividing the $200 paid by the thirty shares purchased results in a $6.65 average per-share price. You can see how dollar-cost averaging lowers the cost overall and allows you to accumulate wealth without spending more.

Now let's look at the reverse scenario.

During retirement, most people take a set amount of capital out of their portfolio each month to cover costs. This is the opposite of what they do during their working lives, when they are putting a set amount in each month. So, what does this do to a portfolio? Let's look at an example.

Say a retiree has an $800,000 portfolio made up of eight thousand shares of stock. They need $6,000 each month to cover living expenses and retirement fun. Maybe they are getting $2,000 from Social Security. That means they need $4,000 from their portfolio. If they are like many people, their portfolio is set up for growth, not income. They might be able to generate $1,000 a month in income, but they need to sell $3,000 worth of shares to cover the shortfall.

The first month they sell shares, each share is priced at $100, so they only need to sell thirty shares. But the next month, the price falls to $75 per share. Now they need to sell forty shares. Uh-oh. The market continues to go down. Next month they need to sell fifty shares. A few more months of ups and downs, and by the end of the year, the retiree has sold five hundred shares. The retiree doesn't think too much about this. After all, they still have seventy-five hundred shares left.

But as the years go on, inflation begins to drive up monthly expenses. The retiree might need expensive medical care. It isn't long before they are selling six hundred or seven hundred shares a year. In less than ten years, the retirement principal could be less than half what it started at. Plus, the retiree probably needs to take out even more than they had originally anticipated because expenses have gone up. This does not bode well for the next few years. Any retiree who continues on this path is committing financial suicide. They are slip-sliding down Mount Everest, and the end result is not pretty. This is often the time when someone walks through my door.

I can hear you saying that you understand you are dipping into principal, but you are confident that at the rate you are spending it, you will be just fine. What you might not understand is that the depletion doesn't occur at a steady rate. It often is exponential. Taking the same amount out of your portfolio often depletes it faster than investing the same amount that grew it.

Picture a snowball during the two different life phases. During the accumulation phase, that snowball starts small. It's hard to push it up Accumulation Hill, but you can see that it is slowly getting bigger, so you put in the effort. As you add savings and investments, it gets bigger and bigger until it reaches the peak of the hill. You are still putting in the effort, but as the snowball crests the hill, it begins to pick up speed. It hits a few rocks and loses a bit of snow here and there, but it has taken on a life of its own. Nothing can stop its growing. And the more it grows, the faster it grows. By the time it reaches the bottom of Accumulation Hill, it is huge.

You rush down the hill and admire how it has grown. Then you realize that you are at the top of Retirement Hill. You say to yourself, "My snowball is big, but I'd like it bigger. My method of growing this snowball worked so well on Accumulation Hill that I'll use it again on Retirement Hill." In fact, since you are at the top of Retirement Hill, it is all downhill from here, so you assume it will continue to grow just as it always has.

But Retirement Hill is different from Accumulation Hill. It has less snow to pick up. Plus, it is warmer, so the snowball begins to melt. Just as snowballs on Accumulation Hill pick up speed as they go down the hill, those on Retirement Hill also pick up speed. But instead of growing, they begin to shrink. And they shrink faster and faster as they fly down the hill, melting from the heat and losing snow to protruding roots and rocks. Retirement Hill is long, and it is very possible that your snowball will completely disappear before it reaches the bottom. That is not a good outcome.

You need to protect your snowball from the heat and hazards of Retirement Hill. It's not going to protect itself.

Reversing the Equation

You can see how continuing to do what you have always done results in depleting your principal. In other words, you are investing in reverse. But you can take that phrase and make reverse investing a positive by flipping your focus from growth to income. You can make your principal work for you and produce the income you need each month rather than have it dwindle slowly but surely.

Let's go back to the example I gave earlier of the farmer with the hundred acres of fertile but mostly unplowed land. He has spent years accumulating the acreage, but now his needs have changed, and he needs cash rather than land. He can certainly sell some acreage to pay the expenses he needs to pay, which will likely work for a few years. But at some point he will run out of land. A better plan is to make the land work for him. He can plant some of the acreage himself. This will bring him yearly income when he sells the crops at harvest time. If he plants a variety of crops, he can stagger when the harvest income is realized and stagger his income. He can also rent out acreage to fellow farmers for a consistent income that doesn't depend on crop prices. All this will allow him to hold on to his acreage and let it increase in value until he is ready to sell it. He won't be under pressure to sell at a discount because his living expenses are being covered by the crop and rental income. He is in a win-win situation.

Your investment portfolio should be set up the same way. Let the principal work for you by providing income. It can be done.

Keep It Simple

At its core, retirement is about income. It's really not complicated. But there is a bit more to it. It's about having *consistent* income that covers your expenses month in and month out.

If you go back to historical S&P 500 returns, you'll see that from 1926 to 1992, the average annual return was about 10 percent. You might wonder why I chose those years. During those decades, dividends were a primary reason for investing in stocks. In fact, almost half the return during those years' returns was from dividends—48 percent to be exact.[20]

---

20   Stock market returns between 1926 and 1992, Official Data, https://www.officialdata.org/us/stocks/s-p-500/1926?amount=100&endYear=1992.

$100 in S&P 500, 1926-1992

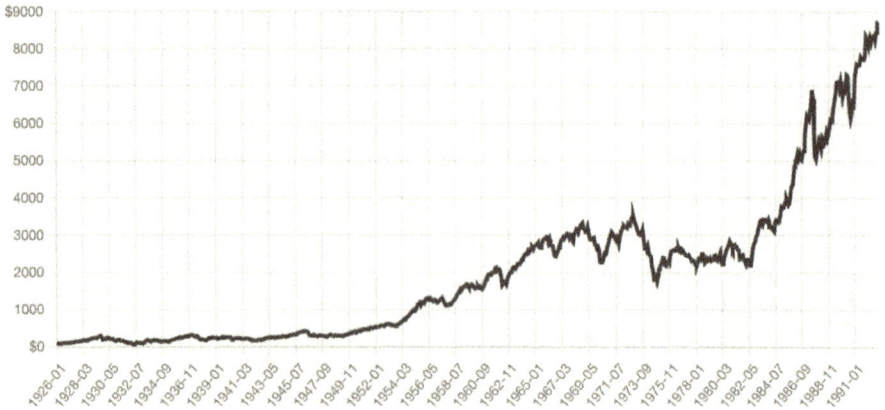

"S&P 500: $100 in 1926 → $69,191.05 in 1992," Official Data, accessed May 7, 2024, https://www.officialdata.org/us/stocks/s-p-500/1926?amount= 100&endYear=1992.

As you can see from the chart, if an investor had bought $100 worth of stock in 1926 and let it ride until 1992, investing all the dividends along the way, they would end up with more than $69,000 sixty-six years later. About $33,120 would have come in the form of dividends. Putting money into dividend stocks was the way nearly everyone invested in the 1960s and 1970s. You would have been hard pressed to find any investor who didn't own shares of IBM or AT&T. Investors in the 1960s and 1970s didn't realize they were investing for income, but they actually were, simply because of how the market was structured.

Then in the 1980s and 1990s, the high-flying tech stocks took over, and investors began concentrating on growth. No one wanted to miss out on doubling their money overnight. Clipping coupons and investing for income was for old fogeys. And the growth lovers actually had a good run. But you can't count on growth year in and year out, and most of us remember the dot-com crash. Investing for income doesn't mean you have to give up growth. It simply means you focus on conservative growth. By focusing on the old-fashioned method of investing in conservative, dividend-paying stocks, you can get solid growth gains while also realizing consistent income returns.

The benefits of investing in long-term, dividend-paying stocks are similar to those of a landlord who owns a $100,000 rental property that generates $12,000 a year in rent. The owner can focus on the multiple listings to estimate the worth of his property and celebrate as it goes up in value. But does that change his bottom line? No. Can he spend it? No. But look at the rental income. That is cash flow he can count on month in and month out.

Imagine collecting $12,000 a year for ten years on that same $100,000 property! That landlord can count on the rental income, but he will probably also see the property increase in value. There may be a time in ten, fifteen, or twenty years when he wants to sell the property. Because he has control of his property, he can sell when it is most advantageous to do so. This is an important point. You don't want to sell when the market is down. And retirees shouldn't be dipping into their principal to pay ongoing expenses, forcing them to sell shares at inopportune times.

Hanging on to your principal will also provide an inflation hedge against future increases in living expenses. Starting to spend the principal at eighty-five is a much different scenario than spending it at sixty-five. At eighty-five, your money likely only needs to last another ten years or so. At sixty-five, it might have to last thirty years. That's why it's so important to invest for income. That's why it's so important to shift to the distribution phase so that when you get to your later years, you'll still have your principal to spend if you need an inflation hedge or have unexpected healthcare expenses.

For many retirees, seeing the principal remain intact gives them peace of mind that makes their retirement years more pleasant. No one likes seeing their balances go down. The number one fear for an American retiree is running out of money before they run out of breath. Number two is being a burden on their children.

If you wind up investing in reverse because you don't realize you're spending principal every year, eventually you probably will run out of money before you run out of breath and be a burden on your children. And I don't know of anyone who wants that to happen!

When you invest with the goal of preserving principal, you are increasing your batting average and making your money last longer. You aren't looking to hit a home run. You are picking and choosing the balls to swing at to get on base. The markets might go up and down, but if you are consistently getting $50,000 from a $1 million portfolio, market fluctuations don't matter. It doesn't bother you if the market is down. The dividends and interest payments continue to fund your lifestyle. Retirees who have an income-centric portfolio continue to do whatever they were doing before a market downturn. No one wants to have to change their life each year depending on what the market is doing.

The changes made in retirement do not need to be huge. Small movements in a boat rudder can result in keeping a boat on course or quickly changing courses if necessary. That's the same way it is when it comes to retirement. You want to make that minor change of flipping the G and the I so you are investing for income and can get the most mileage out of your money.

QUICK TAKES

- Reverse investing can have two meanings. One will deplete your principal and leave you cash poor. The other will focus on income instead of growth and provide a more secure retirement.

- Focusing on income isn't hard. Keep it simple. Invest the old-fashioned way.

- When you invest for income, the chickens might get skinnier during a market downturn, but they are still laying eggs.

Social Security is not just another government spending program.

It is a promise from generation to generation.

–HANK JOHNSON

CHAPTER 6

MAXIMIZING SOCIAL SECURITY

Social Security is a vital spoke in the most important wheel of retirement, which is the wheel of income. In my meetings with clients, the number one fear they have is running out of money before the end of their lives. How you choose to collect this benefit plays a key role in planning your retirement.

Here's something to think about. When you look at different methods of taking Social Security, sometimes the difference between the number one and number two best ways of collecting it could be as much as $100,000 or more of additional benefits over the course or your lifetime, from a system you've already paid into throughout your working years. In other words, this one decision could be one of the most important decisions you make as you prepare for retirement.

We help our clients get the most income from all their sources to maximize their benefits. When looking at the big picture, it's about organizing all your assets, not just looking at Social Security in a vacuum. Keep in mind that the best problem to have in retirement is always having more income than you need … imagine that! No retiree will ever complain to their advisor for helping them achieve too much income.

It is critical that you have a professionally trained advisor on your side who is well versed in Social Security and has the software that determines the right time to maximize your benefits. When wisely used in conjunction with all available income sources, i.e., 401(k)s and IRAs, this software has allowed me to help many clients obtain more benefits. Here is an example.

Several years ago, a couple came to my office, and the husband was contemplating the best time to retire. He was sixty-four years old at that time and his wife was sixty-six, and he was eager to retire within a few months. Once I gathered their financial data, including their Social Security benefits based on their age, we decided together that what was best for her was to take her benefits now and for him to delay his until full retirement age (FRA). Doing so allowed them to collect an additional $11,000 more per year. We structured their portfolio in a way that allowed them to have their cake and eat it too.

You can think about your Social Security benefits as the "harvest" you are reaping from the years you have paid into the fund. You have been planting "seeds" over time, which have been growing year after year. Now you're ready to harvest your "crop." But before you do, ask yourself a question: Is it better for you to take an *early harvest* that will limit your return? Or should you delay your harvest and let your crop *mature* longer and yield a better result? Here's what I mean.

You can take your Social Security benefits as early as age sixty-two, and for some people that makes sense. However, you will be limiting your monthly check to its current amount for the rest of your life. But if you delay taking your benefits until FRA or even age seventy, you will increase your monthly benefit, giving you a better financial quality of life in your latter years. Here's a good example:[21]

---

21   US Social Security Administration, "When to Start Receiving Retirement Benefits," Publication No. 05-10147, January 2023, https://www.ssa.gov/pubs/EN-05-10147.pdf.

Let's say you turn 62 in 2023, your full retirement age is 67, and your monthly benefit that starts at full retirement age is $1,000. If you start to get benefits at age 62, we'll reduce your monthly benefit 30 percent to $700 to account for the longer time you receive benefits. This decrease is usually permanent. If you choose to delay your receipt of benefits until age 70, you would increase your monthly benefit to $1,240. This increase is the result of delayed retirement credits you earn for your decision to postpone receipt of benefits past your full retirement age. The benefit at age 70 in this example is about 77 percent more than the benefit you would receive each month if you start to get benefits at age 62—a difference of $540 each month.

While each person must decide what is best for their financial situation and life circumstances, I always encourage my clients to give serious consideration to delaying their Social Security. For most people, having an extra $540 each month to do with as they please is a welcome "harvest." As I tell my clients, you have to think objectively, not emotionally. Don't get caught up in the present, but think about the future. In the context of your Social Security, if you focus only on the here and now, you might be disappointed years down the road. Once you decide to take your benefits early, you can't go back. To illustrate, consider the following chart:

Monthly Benefit Amounts Differ Based on the Age You Decide to Start Receiving Benefits

This example assumes a benefit of $1,000 at a full retirement age of 67

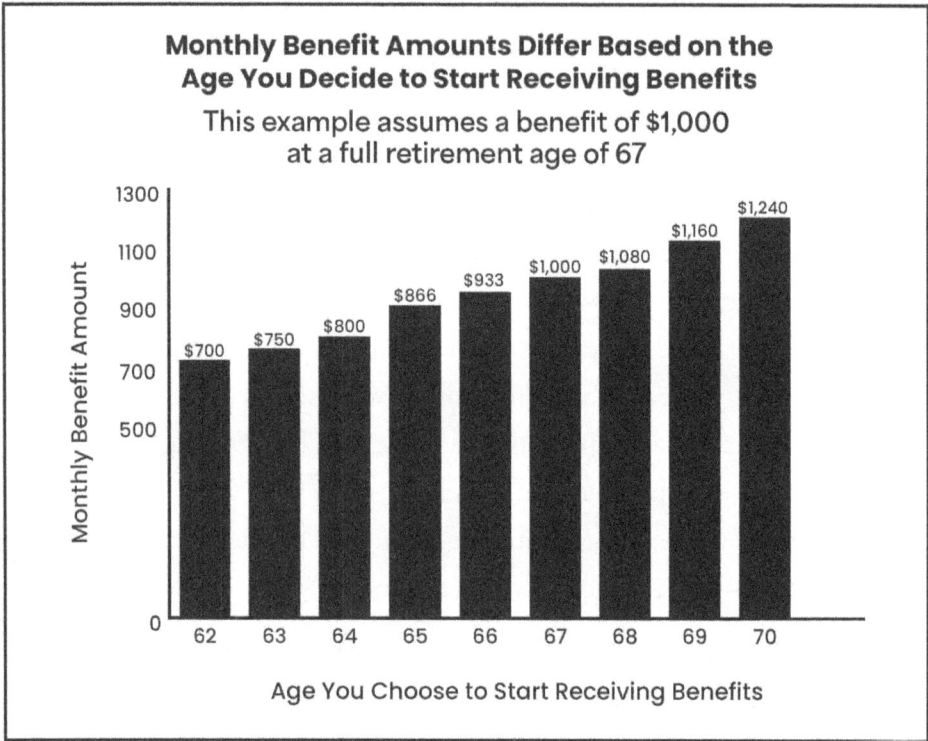

US Social Security Administration, "When to Start Receiving Retirement Benefits," Publication No. 05-10147. January 2023, https://www.ssa.gov/pubs/EN-05-10147.pdf.

Here's another illustration:

Comparing Best Ages to Take Social Security
(Using a 5% investment return)

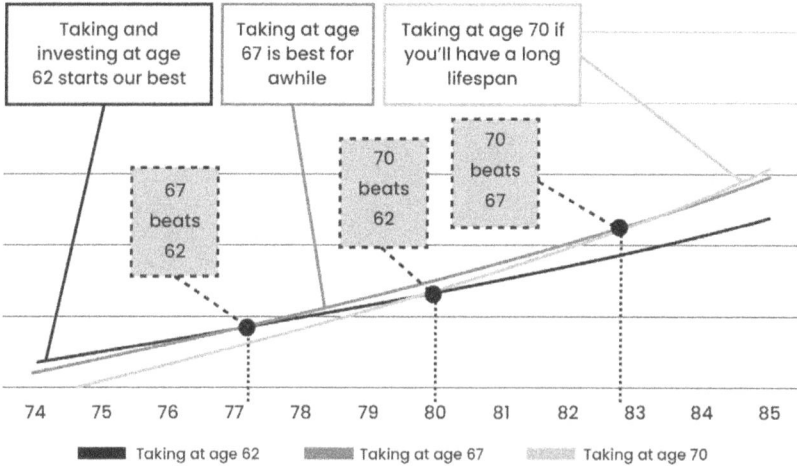

| Taking and investing at age 62 starts our best | Taking at age 67 is best for awhile | Taking at age 70 if you'll have a long lifespan |

67 beats 62

70 beats 62

70 beats 67

74 75 76 77 78 79 80 81 82 83 84 85

■ Taking at age 62   ■ Taking at age 67   ▨ Taking at age 70

Bottom line: if you take early Social Security, you need to make sure you have saved enough in your portfolio to make up the difference versus delaying your benefits.

■ ■ ■

Throughout the United States, Social Security has become an "inalienable right" for all American citizens. And for individuals sixty-five and older, it often provides the major part of their income, making these benefits critical to their financial wellness. In 2024, an average of almost sixty-eight million Americans per month will receive a Social Security benefit, totaling about $1.5 trillion in benefits paid during the year.[22] Since August 14, 1935, when the act was drafted during President Franklin D. Roosevelt's first term and signed into law, countless people have depended upon this government benefit to help them through their retirement years. Therefore, no matter the size of a client's portfolio, every financial plan must include a discussion about Social Security.

However, since its inception—and even more so in the twenty-first century—many myths have been propagated. Let's take a look at some of these and then bring in some sanity and reason.

MYTH #1: Social Security will run out of money.

Social Security is part of a larger trust fund called OASDI, or Old-Age, Survivors, and Disability Insurance. As long as there are payroll taxes, Social Security will not run out of money. You can consider it a pay-as-you-go system; the revenue generated from the Federal Insurance Contributions Act (FICA) and Self-Employed Contributions Act (SECA) taxes largely cover the Social Security benefits being paid out.

Having said that, Social Security will face funding challenges. For the past decades, more money has been collected than has been paid out, with a surplus of $2.83 trillion by the end of 2022.[23] However, with the retiree population growing faster than the working population and living longer lives than past generations, the system is now paying out more than it brings in. Projections show that Social

---

22 US Social Security Administration, "Fact Sheet: Social Security," accessed May 8, 2024, https://www.ssa.gov/news/press/factsheets/basicfact-alt.pdf.

23 US Social Security Administration, "Trust Fund Data," accessed May 8, 2024, https://www.ssa.gov/policy/trust-funds-summary.html.

Security will run out of money by 2037 (contrary to many reports that state 2034).[24]

HERE'S THE TRUTH.

The Social Security trust fund is designed to collect tax revenue and pay benefits. However, it will only collect enough to pay around 80 percent of scheduled benefits based on the latest estimate. To change this outcome would take an act of Congress—literally. As it did in 1983, when Social Security reserves were almost depleted, Congress would need to take steps to shore up the trust fund's finances. Back then, these steps included the following:

- Raising the FRA

- Increasing the payroll tax rate

- Introducing an income tax on benefits

Will the government allow Social Security to run out of money? No … not unless every politician wants to be run out of the country! Will the government shore up the trust fund? Certainly. However, when and how they do so remain distant decisions.

MYTH #2: Social Security is tax-free.

Until 1984, Americans never paid taxes on Social Security benefits.

---

24   Stephen C. Goss, "The Future Financial Status of the Social Security Program," Social Security Bulletin 70, no. 3 (2010), https://www.ssa.gov/policy/docs/ssb/v70n3/v70n3p111.html.

HERE'S THE TRUTH.

In 1983, Social Security was overhauled by Congress, with President Reagan making a portion of Social Security benefits taxable, depending on an individual's income level.

Today, the federal government charges taxes on up to 50 percent of Social Security benefits for couples filing jointly with an annual income between $32,000 and $44,000 and for individuals with an income of $25,000 to $34,000. For incomes above either of these thresholds, 85 percent of benefits are taxable.

Also, if you live in one of the following states, it is possible that you might owe state taxes on your Social Security income:

- Colorado

- Connecticut

- Kansas

- Minnesota

- Missouri

- Montana

- Nebraska

- New Mexico

- Rhode Island

- Vermont

- Utah

- West Virginia

MYTH #3: You should take Social Security as soon as you can get it.

This is most often driven by Myth #1.

HERE'S THE TRUTH.

Deciding when to take Social Security depends on each individual's circumstance. Depending on when you were born, you can start collecting as early as age sixty-two, or you might decide to wait until your full retirement age or age seventy based on your work history. FRA is factored as follows:

- Born in 1954 or earlier: You've already hit FRA
- Born in 1955: Age sixty-six and two months
- Born in 1956: Age sixty-six and four months
- Born in 1957: Age sixty-six and six months
- Born in 1958: Age sixty-six and eight months
- Born in 1959: Age sixty-six and ten months
- Born in 1960 or later: Age sixty-seven

Keep in mind that if you decide to take Social Security retirement benefits early, your benefit will be permanently reduced.

MYTH #4: Nonworking spouses will not receive Social Security benefits.

For spouses who have been stay-at-home moms and dads, the thought of having no income of their own in retirement can be frightening. Social Security provides benefits to not only retired workers but also to spouses who may not have contributed to the program. Many families have single-family earners who have solely contributed to Social Security.

HERE'S THE TRUTH.

Even if the spouse has never worked, they may be eligible for Social Security benefits if they are at least sixty-two years old and the working spouse is receiving retirement or disability benefits. These are known as "SSA spousal benefits." In most situations, the working spouse must file for their own Social Security benefit before their partner can claim spousal benefits. As well, the spouse must be at least sixty-two years of age and married to the primary beneficiary. It is also important to know that spousal benefits are capped at half the previously working spouse's benefit at full retirement age.[25]

MYTH #5: Social Security benefits will be cut in half when one spouse dies.

No one want to talk about, or even consider, the death of a spouse. But it is 100 percent guaranteed that everyone will die at some point.

---

25   "Family Benefits," Social Security Administration, accessed June 1, 2023, https://www.ssa.gov/benefits/retirement/planner/applying7.html.

For the spouse who has been a stay-at-home provider, losing the full benefits of their partner's Social Security is a fearful thought.

HERE'S THE TRUTH.

When the primary Social Security beneficiary dies, the surviving spouse is eligible for survivor benefits. The percentage of survivor benefits is a complex formula of the deceased spouse's Social Security benefits combined with the surviving spouse's age at the time they start receiving benefits. For example, if the surviving spouse is at FRA, they can receive 100 percent of the deceased spouse's benefit amount. If the surviving spouse is between age sixty and FRA, they can receive a reduced amount of the deceased spouse's benefit. If the surviving spouse is disabled, they can receive survivor benefits as early as age fifty.

Keep the following in mind:

- The surviving spouse will not receive a survivor benefit in addition to their own retirement benefit. Social Security will pay the higher of the two amounts.

- If the surviving spouse is not at FRA and is still working, their survivor benefit could be affected by Social Security's earning limit.

- Whether or not the surviving spouse worked long enough to qualify for their own Social Security benefits, this individual can still collect benefits on the deceased spouse's work record.

MYTH #6: You can take Social Security at age sixty-two and still work as much as you want.

When people are getting close to their retirement, they see Social Security as an "add-on" income while they are still working. However, they don't realize that taking their benefits at age sixty-two severely limits their ability to earn work-related income.

HERE'S THE TRUTH.

If you take social security at age sixty-two, or any age prior to FRA, then you're limited in the amount of income you can earn while working. If your working income exceeds this limited amount, you have to pay back one dollar for every two dollars you collect from your Social Security benefits.[26]

MYTH #7: Social Security income will be enough to retire on.

Back in 2012, I noticed that every widow I met with in their late seventies was living solely on their Social Security benefits. Their stories were all similar: when they retired from work, they took Social Security benefits at age sixty-two. At that time their husband was still alive, so there were two checks coming in every month. At first they thought the combined amount of income was more than enough to live on. They didn't even have any debt; this generation was more frugal than today's generation. By the time I met with one particular

---

26 "What Happens if I Work and Get Social Security Retirement Benefits?," Social Security Administration, accessed June 1, 2023, https://faq.ssa.gov/en-us/Topic/article/KA-01921.

widow, she was inquiring about a reverse mortgage and wanted to know my thoughts. When you think about it, what is the last asset you can rely on when you're out of money? Your home!

To me, it is inconceivable that people today think they can live on their Social Security benefits. According to IRS data, the average Social Security payout for retirees as of September 2023 was $1,841.27. Spouses of retired workers drew an average check of $888.03.[27]

HERE'S THE TRUTH.

Even if Social Security receives a massive makeover from Congress, American citizens should *never* consider the program a sufficient retirement plan. On average, Social Security provides about 40 percent of a beneficiary's preretirement earnings.[28] If you want to live comfortably in retirement, you'll need to boost your retirement savings as much as possible, pay down your debt, and keep your spending in check. You'll also need to consider Social Security as an "extra" income that supplements your retirement planning.

If you plan on making Social Security your main source of income and you plan on taking your benefits between age sixty-two and before your full retirement age, consider this: you are already taking a 30 percent reduction. Now think about this: in order to keep Social Security solvent, one of the cost savings the government is weighing is to reduce overall benefits by 20 percent. If you do the math, that's a potential 50 percent reduction in your benefits!

---

27   John Csiszar, "How Big Is the Average Social Security Check of a Retiree Living in Poverty?," Nasdaq, December 31, 2023, accessed May 8, 2024, https://www.nasdaq.com/articles/how-big-is-the-average-social-security-check-of-a-retiree-living-in-poverty.

28   Andrew G. Biggs and Glenn R. Springstead, "Alternate Measures of Replacement Rates for Social Security Benefits and Retirement Income," Social Security Bulletin 68, no. 2 (2008), accessed May 8, 2024, https://www.ssa.gov/policy/docs/ssb/v68n2/v68n2p1.html.

You might be thinking, *If I take early benefits during my "go-go" years (the years I'm still very active), by the time I'm in my "slow-go" years (the years in which I live a more sedentary lifestyle), and then move into my "no-go" years (the years in which I am content staying home and working in my garden), I won't need a lot of money.* The trouble with this type of thinking is that it doesn't factor in inflation.

To illustrate, if groceries cost $1,000 in 2015, those same groceries would cost $1,301.24 today, an increase of $301.24 over nine years. The dollar had an average inflation rate of 2.97 percent per year between 2015 and today, producing a cumulative price increase of 30.12 percent. This means that today's prices are 1.30 times higher than in 2015, according to the Bureau of Labor Statistics consumer price index. A dollar today only buys 76.850 percent of what it could buy back then.[29] Now, project those numbers out for the next ten, twenty, or thirty years, and you can see how inflation will deplete your financial resources without you spending one extra dollar.

Pros and Cons

Now let's take a look at some of the pros and cons of taking Social Security early.[30]

---

29   "CPI Inflation Calculator," In2013Dollars.com, accessed May 8, 2024, https://www. in2013dollars.com/us/inflation/2015?amount=1000.

30   "Exempt Amounts under the Earnings Test," Social Security Administration, accessed May 8, 2024, https://www.ssa.gov/oact/cola/rtea.html.

Keep Working: Understand the Annual Earnings Test

If you apply for Social Security before full retirement age and you work:

- $1 in benefits will be withheld for every $2 you earn over $22,320 in 2024

- Benefit will be adjusted at full retirement age

- Don't let the annual earnings test discourage you from working

- To avoid the earnings test, wait until full retirement age or later to apply for benefits

Decisions, Decisions

Throughout my years as a financial advisor, I've had countless conversations with individuals concerning the advantages and disadvantages of taking their Social Security benefit before their FRA. The main advantage is being able to collect benefits for a longer period of time. The main disadvantage is that the benefit amount will be reduced.

While each individual's situation is different, a key point to remember is that delaying your benefits until after full retirement age makes you eligible for delayed retirement credits that would increase your monthly benefit. However, keep in mind that the benefit increase stops when you reach age seventy.

Here are a couple of key points to keep in mind:

- If you've already reached full retirement age, you can start receiving benefits before the month you apply. However, you cannot receive retroactive benefits for any month *before* you reached FRA or more than six months in the past.

- If you retire before age seventy, some of your delayed retirement credits won't be applied until the January *after* you start receiving benefits.

When Should You Start Receiving Your Benefits?

I can tell you unequivocally that every client asks me this question. I can also tell you that there is no "ideal age" for everyone because each person's financial situation is unique. However, there are some important factors to consider, such as the following:

- If your financial planning includes your continuing to work while receiving Social Security, there are set limits on how much you can earn each year between age sixty-two and full retirement age and still receive your benefits. However, once you reach FRA, your earnings do not affect your benefits. While no one knows how long they will live, it is important to have some guidelines as per the following chart:[31]

---

31 Worldometer, "Life Expectancy of the World Population," accessed May 8, 2024, https://www.worldometers.info/demographics/life-expectancy/.

LIFE EXPECTANCY

Source: 2015 Intergenerational Report

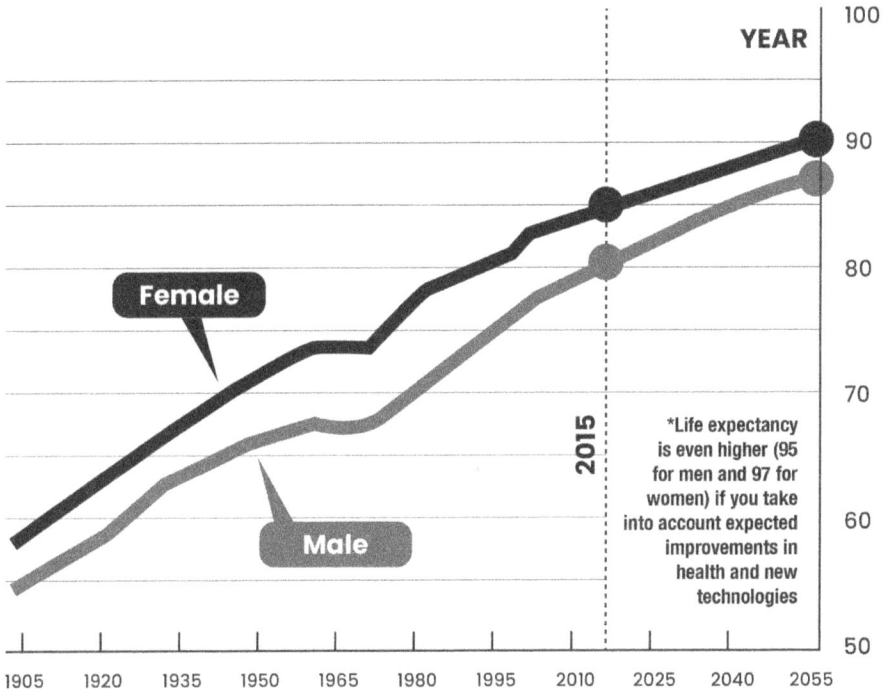

Worldometer, "Life Expectancy of the World Population," accessed May 8, 2024, https://www.worldometers.info/demographics/life-expectancy/.

- You may qualify for benefits as a widow, widower, or surviving divorced spouse on another record, and you can apply for survivors benefits now and delay your retirement benefit until later.

- If you have other sources of income, you can increase the value of your benefits by investing instead of spending your additional income.

- Once you start receiving Social Security retirement benefits, some members of your family may also qualify to receive benefits on your record. For example, your spouse or a child can receive a monthly payment of up to one-half your full retirement Social Security benefit, and these payments will not decrease your retirement benefit.

Wrapping Up

There is no doubt that Social Security benefits are one of the most important sources of US retirement income. In fact, a combined three surveys conducted by SSA.gov report that roughly half the aged population live in households that receive at least 50 percent of total family income from Social Security and that about one-quarter of the aged live in households that receive at least 90 percent of family income from Social Security.[32] I would advocate that with proper financial planning, you don't have to make these benefits your primary source of income. In fact, with sound planning, these benefits can be a source of discretionary spending that you can use to bless others with, take a trip you've always wanted, or help your family in unexpected ways.

QUICK TAKES

- Think about your Social Security benefits as the "harvest" you are reaping from the years you have paid into the fund.
- You can take your Social Security benefits as early as age sixty-two, and for some people that makes sense.

---

32 "Social Security Basic Facts," Social Security Administration, accessed June 1, 2023, https://www.ssa.gov/news/press/factsheets/basicfact-alt.pdf.

However, you will be limiting your monthly check to its current amount for the rest of your life. If your working income exceeds this limited amount, you have to pay back one dollar for every two dollars you collect from your Social Security benefits.

- Will the government allow Social Security to run out of money? No ... not unless every politician wants to be run out of the country! Will the government shore up the trust fund? Certainly. However, when and how they do so remain distant decisions.

- On average, Social Security provides about 40 percent of a beneficiary's preretirement earnings. If you want to live comfortably in retirement, you'll need to boost your retirement savings as much as possible, pay down your debt, and keep your spending in check.

- If you plan on making Social Security your main source of income and you plan on taking your benefits at age sixty-two and before your full retirement age, consider this: you are already taking a 30 percent reduction. Now think about this: in order to keep Social Security solvent, one of the cost savings the government is weighing is to reduce overall benefits by 20 percent. If you do the math, that's a potential 50 percent reduction in your benefits!

If you win with money, it doesn't mean someone else has to lose.

You can create value where none existed.

—DAVE RAMSEY

CHAPTER 7

WIN, DIVIDE, AND CONQUER

Now that you've arrived at this chapter, you might be thinking that you can live off Social Security alone. If so, then this chapter may not be important to you. But if you're like the majority of those who come into my office, you realize that Social Security alone will not afford you the ability to enjoy retirement and do the things you want to do. This chapter will show you how to bridge that gap between your Social Security benefits and what you need to live comfortably, based on the more than twenty years of experience I have in the industry.

As you already know, your retirement financial foundation starts with Social Security, your 401(k), perhaps a pension, and maybe other sources of income such as a rental property. Like most people, you've spent thirty-plus years working hard to build your net worth. And like most people, you want to make sure your investments and income outlast you throughout your retirement. However, with the volatility in interest rates, the continual rise in inflation, and the unpredictability of the markets, it's more important than ever to have a comprehensive financial strategy. But what does that look like?

Purpose-Based versus Performance-Based Investing[33]

During the early retirement years, what I call the "go-go" years, most people are spending money and enjoying the freedom from the nine-to-five workday. If they've planned well, they will be fulfilling their bucket list, which might include traveling, purchasing an RV, spoiling their grandchildren, or helping their children. During the go-go years, the priority is on *purpose-based investing*, with a focus on creating as much income as possible.

However, by the time most people reach age eighty and beyond, life is starting to become more sedentary, and your money needs to serve a purpose: to generate income. At this point for the majority of retirees, *performance-based investing* becomes priority, with the goal of making sure their retirement income will cover costs such as living in a retirement community, covering medical expenses, and/or receiving care in a nursing home.

The last thing anyone wants to experience is running out of money before their life ends! And this can easily happen when an individual starts spending more and more of their principal. Certainly, spending a little of their principal to hedge against inflation can be a good thing to do. However, the more principal that is used up, the less income there will be to cover any major expenses.

During your performance-based investing years, an astute financial advisor will tell you about the benefits of "dollar-cost averaging." Dollar-cost averaging is a strategy that focuses on investing a set amount of money at regular intervals, regardless of the price of the investment instrument. The goal is to mitigate price volatility

---

33 Performance-based investing is most important when accumulating wealth, but once retirement planning is the goal, then purpose-based investing focuses on income first and growth second.

and lower the average cost per share. However, during retirement, whenever you tap into your principal, it's akin to "reverse dollar-cost averaging" because you are selling at whatever the market determines is a fair value and reducing your original investment.

Consider the following analogy.

You own a thirty-unit condominium building that you've been collecting rent on and also paying off for years, and now you own it free and clear. Each apartment represents one year of your retirement savings. Let's say you decide to sell one condo each year, with the hope that inflation will drive up the price of the next unit you will sell. You do this every year until the twenty-ninth year. Now you have only one condo left, and you're still living.

The question now becomes this: How much did your last condo grow in value? Is it worth enough to cover your remaining years? Is it worth enough to cover your medical expenses and your living expenses? I would suggest that is very doubtful. There is no way to predict how much you will need to live on in future years, what your health will be like, and what the value of your last condo unit will be.

Unfortunately, many financial advisors today will tell you to follow the above analogy. The problem is, whether your investments are in mutual funds, individual stocks, bonds, money markets, CDs, or any other asset, by selling that asset, or even a portion of it, you are setting yourself up for diminished returns for the rest of your life. You are reducing your principal slowly but surely.

Keep in mind that your portfolio is made up of ownership called shares that you own in the aforementioned investments. If the income that comes from interest or dividends from your investments is not enough to compensate for your withdrawals, then you will be selling shares. When markets go up, you sell fewer shares, and when they go down, you sell more of them. Imagine doing this every month and every year for the rest of your life. The problem is that you run the risk of running out of money before the end of your life.

The Good News

Instead of slowly cannibalizing your principal, here's a better idea that illustrates purpose-based investing via the condo building analogy. Why not continue renting out each of your thirty condos and maintain ownership of the building instead of selling each unit? Doing so means you are preserving your main asset, the building itself. What if the condos go down in value? That doesn't affect you because you're still collecting rent. What if they go up in value? That's great, because you have the option to sell one or two units—i.e., perhaps you want to financially help one of your kids—while still owning the majority of your condos.

The good news is, there are purpose-based investments that can make you as financially successful as the performance-based investments that set you up for retirement. Purpose-based investing allows you to retire and stay retired! It shifts the focus from *accumulation* to *distribution*. Distribution focuses on things such as dividend income, which you can use to fund your lifestyle without tapping into the principal.

Now, here is the struggle that most people face: they don't like change. But if you are going to "win" throughout your retirement, then you must "divide and conquer."

Here's what I mean.

To "win" throughout your retirement means you must invest *intentionally* for the phase you're in. "Divide and conquer" comes into play by being honest with yourself as to what stage of retirement you are in and choosing to make different decisions as needed. To do this, you need an investment advisor who is strategic in their planning and who can help you "divide and conquer" your own subjective thinking. Unfortunately, because most people are resistant to change, they would rather leave their retirement portfolio as is. Even worse, many of the well-known investment companies don't even recognize the need to switch from performance-based to purpose-based investments, so they never address the need to divide and conquer.

Let's bring this back to your financial situation and the condo analogy. Your portfolio is not made up of condos; it's made up of investment instruments such as mutual funds, bond funds, and/or individual stocks. If you sell any of your instruments, you have a capital gain for that particular year, but you lose future income for good. However, if you're working with a wise financial advisor who specializes in investing your portfolio for income in a similar way to collecting rent from the condos, you will always have *increased* income to cover your living expenses.

Think about this. Let's say your portfolio is worth $1 million (this would be the same as the thirty-unit condo building). If each of your thirty assets within your portfolio (i.e., each condo unit) was conservatively making 2 percent, you would have a net income of around $20,000 per year (interest and dividends). That might be a good return except for one thing: your advisor's management fee is typically 1 percent, or $10,000, meaning your true net income is around $10,000 (management fees are great for the financial advisor, but they have a negative effect on every portfolio, to the point that they can turn a double-digit return into single digits). Therefore, if you need $50,000 per year of income, you will be forced to take withdrawals from your principal. This is akin to being forced to sell a condo, which is similar to selling shares.

In addition, many investment companies and managers use what I call a "cookie cutter" approach to managing a portfolio. When a client is working with a financial advisor who is employed by one of the "big name" investment houses, the advisor asks the client if they are an aggressive, conservative, or somewhere-in-between investor when setting financial goals. The advisor then uses a "template" portfolio that matches the goals. The first problem is that clients rarely know what type of investor they really are. The second problem with having a template approach is that no two people have the same life history or financial goals. It's a given that everyone wants to minimize their downside and maximize their upside. For example, if you are a conversative investor, they have a template of funds for your investments. If you're more aggressive, there is another template of funds. In my opinion, this takes the originality and science out of investing for each client. It's a great approach for the company but a lousy one for the client.

■ ■ ■

Let's go back to the equation I referred to in chapter 3: G (Growth) + I (Income) = TR (Total Returns).

$$G + I = TR$$

After accumulating growth over your years of investment, once you're in your retirement years, your focus should switch to income so that you can live off the percentage that your investments have been making for you instead of the investments themselves. This is a good example of "divide and conquer" because you are switching your mindset from performance-based to purpose-based investing. The goal is to preserve your assets, allowing you to gain a monthly income while simultaneously getting some potential growth. While your total returns may not be as great as during your investment years—you are no longer putting money into your portfolio—you now have income that will support your retirement lifestyle and goals. Having income is the name of the game in retirement because it allows you to preserve your assets.

Here's an example. Let's say you need $50,000 per year to live comfortably. These are your choices:

1. Take the money from your principal.

2. Take the money from I or income.

3. Create your investment returns from a combination of the first two.

The choice you make will depend on the following:

1. The size of your portfolio and your age—for instance, if you have a $5 million portfolio and you are in your eighties, you can afford to take money from your principal because the chances are good that you will die before running out of money.

2. How astute your investments are, meaning that if your I or income is great enough to produce $50,000 per year, then you don't have to touch your principal.

3. You may need to use a combination of principal and income generated, depending on your unique financial situation.

I also know there are times when an individual must take out some of their assets. Perhaps they want to help an adult child get started in life. Maybe they want to take a once-in-a-lifetime trip. When delving into assets comes into play, I recommend no more than a 5 percent yearly reduction in the early years, allowing you to get more "mileage" out of your money. More than that means you start running the risk of not having enough money during your later years.

For instance, let's say you are eighty years old and have lived comfortably for the last twenty years, but now you need to go into a retirement home. However, you don't have enough in your portfolio to cover the costs of the home of your choice because you're taking money out of your principal. Conversely, if you had been spending income only, this would have allowed you a better opportunity to preserve your money for possible home healthcare, including a retirement home of your choice.

If at all possible, you want to avoid letting the state you are living in make decisions for you; you will have limited choices without having enough assets to cover future expensive costs. Preserving assets through purpose-based investing always gives you better options.

Here's something else to consider. Purpose-based investing always takes into consideration what are called "value stocks." Instead of investing that is based only on the dividend to produce the income needed (dividend stocks), value stocks offer the best of two worlds: dividends and growth. Value stocks are classified as companies that are currently trading below what they are really worth and will thus have the potential to provide a superior return.

Breathing Room

Recently I had a couple approach me based on a recommendation from another client. This couple was suspicious about how I could help them, something I fully understand. They had been worried about their investments and had become concerned about every penny they spent. However, after working with my team and then having an initial six-month review, the couple realized they could "breathe a little" and began talking about how they had been missing out on enjoying life. Instead of putting all their interest and dividends back into their portfolio and/or savings account, they had other ideas, such as buying an SUV or RV to travel the country in. Twelve months later, they were ready to travel!

The difference?

No one had shown them that they needed to focus on the income they were making (I) instead of that taking out their foundational assets (G) would affect their total returns (TR).

I've had other clients who, after I showed them they could make up to 70 percent more income, have looked at me like I'm crazy. But I compare what I do to having a "Warren Buffet" mindset versus a "Walmart" mentality. Both will get you what you need, but the former will do so in greater style while leaving much more in your portfolio, which is another illustration of purpose-based investing.

Here's another analogy.

Suppose you heat your house with propane. Whenever your tank goes empty, it costs you money to refill it. But suppose you had solar panels that provided the heat you needed. You would have a continual source of renewable energy that didn't cost you any more than the maintenance of your solar panels. This is the mentality I want to instill in my clients, so they have the confidence to trust me with their portfolios and they can have a new outlook on enjoying life.

It thrills me to see the faces of my clients when they walk through my office door. Their portfolios are still growing, even though they've been taking income all these years. Why? Because we're not selling their portfolio assets. For example, in 2022 when the markets dipped about 30 percent, not one of my clients sold any of their assets. The great thing was that their income was based on years of reinvestment and compounding. And when the markets rebounded—and all markets rebound—the value of their assets had increased, giving them even greater disposable income!

Throughout life, there are two things that are guaranteed to go up: inflation and healthcare costs. Wouldn't it be great if your portfolio were set up so that you have the financial ability to cover both of these? Wouldn't it be great if you could stay in your own home instead of going into a state-funded convalescent home? Wouldn't it be great if you could have your own room in a retirement building instead of having to share a room? When your portfolio is set up to preserve your assets through purpose-based investing *and* provide a solid income, you can then decide when—and if—you need to tap into your principal in order to cover your needs.

Now that's a retirement plan that will be the envy of everyone you know!

Strategies for Divide and Conquer

Throughout your working career, you are in your go-go years. You are constantly on the go, and life seems to fly by at warp speed. Upon retirement, you enter your slow-go years. Life is slowing down, and you are taking time to enjoy family, friends, travel, and other pleasures. On the horizon are your no-go years. This is your golden era in which you have a sedentary lifestyle either at home or in a retirement complex, with the possibility of a convalescent home in your latter years.

From a financial standpoint, your go-go years are focused on wealth creation through high-yield and/or long-term investments. However, during your slow-go years, wealth preservation is priority. And during your no-go years, your thoughts shift toward wealth transfer based on your legal will.

In this section, I will talk about wealth preservation designed to help protect your investments through astute, conversative management that allows for timely withdrawals, inflation protection, and protection of your core assets.

This begs the following question: What are the elements needed in a financial plan to safely guide you through your slow-go years and into your no-go phase of life?

Here's the short answer. For independent financial advisors like me, there is no cookie-cutter, one-size-fits-all approach. Well-planned wealth preservation based on your lifestyle can protect the value of your assets through the use of various financial management and tax strategies. The goal is to achieve financial well-being that gives you peace of mind … and life!

While the particular details of your wealth preservation plan should be worked out with your financial advisor, here are seven strategies that will benefit you in the long run:

1. CREATE A PLAN, SET GOALS, AND DEVELOP A BUDGET BASED ON YOUR PLANNED AND PERIODIC WITHDRAWALS.

You are well aware that each season of your current life has related expenses, and your retirement years are no different. Whether you're a multimillionaire or a multithousandaire, you have to live within your means. Planning is essential, because life does not always go the way you plan. Having and reviewing a plan, goals, and budget allow you to adjust for the unexpected and readjust when necessary. Also, having short-, medium-, and long-term goals in place will help you plan, invest, and budget accordingly.

2. DIVERSIFY, DIVERSIFY, DIVERSIFY!

Financial success is never based on one kind of investment. My twist on the old saying is "Don't put all your financial eggs in one financial basket."

A diversified portfolio means having a healthy mix of assets that may include a combination of stocks, individual bonds, bond-like instruments, cash, real estate, etc. to ensure balanced growth through short- and long-term fluctuations. When you transition into retirement, or if you're already in retirement, your philosophy should shift to more income-producing investing. Keep in mind that you can invest in stocks for growth or income. You can invest in bonds for growth or income. But in retirement, you should focus on stocks and bonds that are income driven *first*. In my opinion, it is best to avoid stock and bond mutual funds, as they force you to spend your principal.

3. SAVE UP TO BUILD AN EMERGENCY FUND OF AT LEAST TWO MONTHS OF LIVING EXPENSES.

This is not money that you keep in your regular checking or savings account. It is best to use a CD or money market account so that you are not tempted to use it for everyday expenses. Ideally, you will continue to build your emergency fund to cover six months' worth of living expenses. Think about this: if you have an emergency, large or small, you'll have the money to cover it without affecting your everyday life. And if you never tap into this fund, you'll have a windfall of your own making!

4. OPTIMIZE YOUR TAX-PLANNING STRATEGIES.

An independent financial advisor can give you solid advice on a variety of ways to minimize your tax liabilities. For example, tax-efficient investments such as tax-deferred individual retirement accounts (IRAs) or 401(k) retirement plans can help minimize your tax burden in the future. For example, while Roth IRAs do not have an up-front tax break, funds can be withdrawn tax-free later in life. During your wealth preservation years, a Roth IRA can help you plan for predictable withdrawals to help sustain your lifestyle.

5. ESTABLISH A REVOCABLE OR IRREVOCABLE TRUST TO HELP YOU GAIN ESTATE TAX ADVANTAGES.

- An **irrevocable trust** transfers the assets from your control to your beneficiary(ies), thereby reducing your estate's value reflected in taxes while protecting your assets from creditors. The caveat: assets in irrevocable trusts cannot be substantively modified because you no longer own the assets. Always remember that the Internal Revenue Service (IRS) changes tax rules periodically, and an astute financial advisor will keep you informed as part of their job in managing your money.

- A **revocable trust** allows loved ones to bypass probate while giving you the opportunity to change the terms at any time. However, this type of trust doesn't protect assets.

If you want asset protection, you must choose an irrevocable trust. It can be possible but usually more difficult to change the terms once you've set them up, but the peace of mind can be well worth it.

Tax rules change over time, so staying abreast of the latest information from the IRS is also key to managing your money.

6. REVIEW AND UPDATE YOUR INSURANCE POLICIES.

- If you've been planning astutely through your go-go years, you have whole, universal, or term life insurance in place.

- Be sure to review your homeowner and auto policies to see what coverages you are entitled to.

- You might have disability insurance, either as a separate policy or through your employer. The point of disability insurance is to help replace your income during times of disability when you cannot do the work in the field in which you were educated. If you have disability insurance or plan on purchasing it, be sure to include something I call "own occupation." This will help protect and cover you in the event you cannot carry out the primary responsibilities of your current job.

- Given that the cost of healthcare is going through the roof, you may have or may want to consider having long-term care insurance to help cover the cost of a home healthcare worker or nursing home. This insurance can help ensure that you don't have to deplete your savings and investments to cover any ongoing expenses.

7. ESTATE PLANNING IS AN IMPORTANT PART OF YOUR FINANCIAL FUTURE.

Estate planning includes a series of legal instruments—including power of attorney, living will, trust, and medical documents—that enable you to pass on your wealth and assets to whomever you desire. It contributes to your wealth preservation by preparing assets for your chosen beneficiaries and helps ensure access continuity to bank accounts and other assets. Be sure to inform anyone who might be affected by your estate plans so that everyone is clear on your plans.

Wrapping Up

I titled this chapter "Win, Divide, and Conquer" because the goal of retirement is to "win" throughout your years, from go-go to slow-go to no-go. When you "divide" your retirement into the "go" years you are in, you can "conquer" your own mindset—with the help of an astute financial advisor—to see money objectively for what it is: a tool to live the life you want to live. Instead of money dictating to you because of your emotional attachment, you can tell your money what to do and how to perform to benefit you the most. Then you will be able to say, "I'm winning" every single day you are alive!

QUICK TAKES

- During the go-go years, the priority is on *performance-based investing*, with a focus on creating as much income as possible. However, by age eighty and beyond, *purpose-based investing* becomes priority, with the goal of making sure that retirement outlasts the end of life.

- To "win" throughout your retirement means you must invest *intentionally* for the phase you're in. "Divide and conquer" comes into play by being honest with yourself as to what stage of retirement you are in and choosing to make different decisions as needed.

- Value stocks offer the best of two worlds: dividends and growth.

- From a financial standpoint, your go-go years are focused on wealth creation while your slow-go years prioritize wealth preservation.

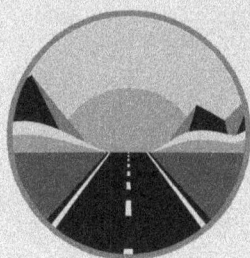

The stock market is filled with individuals who know the price of everything, but the value of nothing.

—PHILLIP FISHER

CHAPTER 8

WORKING WITH A QUALIFIED ADVISOR

N ow that you've made it to this chapter, you're probably curious as to where you can get the type of financial advice that makes sense to you. I cannot stress this enough: it takes only one bad decision to mess up an ideal retirement. In this industry, unfortunately, there are no do-overs.

The first place to start is to find an advisor who is philosophically in line with who you are—a retiree. You're looking for someone who primarily works with preretirees or retirees and is multifaceted in many areas to help you plan for your later years.

Before we get into the qualifications of a financial advisor, I want to say this for the record. As a financial advisor, my experience over the last twenty years has taught me what to recommend and, most importantly, what not to recommend.

As I look back over my early years, I knew very little and was naive. I've recommended many different strategies using mutual funds and ETFs in a passive way and a tactical way. Neither approach sat well with me because I knew the principal was going to be reduced every time a retiree took out income on monthly basis. However, I was smart enough to know I needed something that made more sense. So, I broke old investment habits and learned newer and better habits.

I decided to change to income planning that was basically common sense. I'd always known about using individual stocks and bonds and realized that this investing strategy made the most sense. It was logical and could be individualized and personalized to each client. If I could start my career over, I would use this strategy instead of taking a cookie-cutter approach—i.e., using mutual funds and ETFs as a one-size-fits-all solution.

In the financial industry, there are thousands of people who have degrees or certifications or who work with a big-name company and call themselves "qualified" financial advisors. These "qualified" individuals are ready to tell you how to invest your money, the "best" platforms and vehicles to use, and what the "best" mix of assets is for your portfolio. This begs the following question: What makes these individuals qualified? Is it their degree in finance? Their certifications? The company they work for? And how do they come up with their "best" recommendations for your portfolio?

I realize there are many good advisors who mean well and really do care about the advice they give their clients. But there's only two types of income plan that people will use in retirement: purpose based and performance based. The overall purpose of this book is to let you know there are only two and no more.

Now, you may wonder what I'm talking about, because you may have interviewed four or five advisors and it sounded like each one gave you a different type of plan. Some use retirement planning software; others use past performances like the Monte Carlo analysis, which gives you a range of different market conditions with both bearish and bullish market returns. There are many others that advisors can use.

However, no matter the approach an advisor may use, they all boil down to either purpose-based or performance-based plans.

When you start to tap into your retirement nest egg, assuming you're sticking with performance-based planning, you're going to be taking income each and every month by what we call engineering withdrawals by selling shares (reducing principal) and collecting a combination of interest and dividends to come up with that needed income. Or you can invest in certain select stocks, bonds, and bond-like instruments that will provide you with income and not sell any of your principal, which is purpose-based planning.

If you're like me, you don't like the sound of taking out principal that may have taken you thirty or forty years to accumulate. In other words, paying yourself back your own money seems like it would not last long, and you would run the risk of running out of money faster than if you were just investing for income.

When looking for a financial advisor, the key is to make sure they have been in business for eight to ten years at a minimum. Experience is everything. This business requires so much learning that there's no way an advisor is going to become an expert overnight.

I would suggest that the two most important qualifications are (1) experience and (2) level of independence.

Experience

As the old adage goes, there is no teacher like experience. In the financial world, a qualified and experienced advisor has developed an in-depth knowledge that can include taxes, insurance, Social Security benefits, and of course investment vehicles to suit the needs of their clients. Experience also includes certifications; after all, you wouldn't go to someone with an automotive certification for a health issue or get your roof fixed by a truck driver. A qualified financial advisor might be one or more of the following:

- A Certified Public Accountant (CPA), who can help with taxes and tax planning, financial consulting, and other business services such as mergers and acquisitions

- A Personal Finance Specialist (PFS), who is a CPA and has passed more tests and has more education and experience in financial planning

- A Certified Financial Planner (CFP), who tends to have experience in insurance, taxes, retirement planning, and estate planning

- A Chartered Financial Consultant (ChFC), who has the same knowledge as a CFP and has completed further education consisting of nine college-level courses and has passed a series of course-specific exams

And here's a qualification that is rarely talked about: a love for and passion to help people save and invest for a successful retirement. I've added this for one reason: too many people go into the financial investment business because they feel they can make a lot of money. And that's true! But when they find out the work that is needed, many individuals are quick to leave the industry. Here's a sobering quote to think about: "Financial advisors come into the industry all fired up, thinking they're going to create this massive empire. They think they have everything they need to 'make it.'"[34] And here is another sobering statistic: "The retention rate is low: By the fifth year, only 15–16%

---

34 "The Reality Check: Why Many Financial Advisors Fail and How to Avoid Their Mistakes," The Taylor Method, accessed May 20, 2024, https://www.taylormethod.com/.

of advisors will still be in business. Over 90% of financial advisors in the industry do not last three years. Putting it simply: 9 advisors out of 10 would fail!"[35]

In the business world there's more to owning a business than just owning it. There's more to owning a business than just providing for a family. A business owner has to have a passion for the industry they are in and the customers they serve. Without passion, the inevitable hard times will destroy the confidence of the business owner, and the business will falter soon after. In the financial industry, it is a must for the advisor to be undyingly passionate about helping people save and invest for their golden years of retirement.

Level of Independence

Within the financial services industry, there are countless individuals and companies that promote "always having their client's best interest at heart." But my experience has taught me to question their level of commitment. Now, I'm not putting everyone into the same basket, but once again my experience has proven that when someone works for a bank or a particular investment firm, while they want to do what is *good* for their clients, they also want to do what is *best* for their bank or firm.

Think about this: those who work for a bank or firm are paid by that institution and are paid commissions based on the products and services they sell.

In my opinion, these individuals are biased toward what their institution has to offer because they are incentivized. Why would these people recommend an investment vehicle that is outside their company when doing so means they would lose out on making more

---

35   Ibid.

money? Also, in my opinion, those who work for a bank or institution can take a cookie-cutter approach to their clients. Instead of getting to know each client individually and understanding their needs, they might put conservative clients in a couple of types of investment vehicles and progressive clients in a couple of different vehicles and then call it a day.

A sad fact of the financial advisory world is that people will come in like gangbusters to make lots of money. These individuals have a tendency to build their systems and pigeonhole clients into their company's funds but neglect the clients' personal needs. This makes their clients feel like a small fish in a big pond. It takes six to eight years before a financial advisor *starts* to learn this industry.

Yes, certifications and financial courses help to shorten the learning curve, but I highly recommend *not* hiring an advisor based solely on their education. Why do I say six to eight years? Because a financial advisor needs to know about more than just investing. Clients are looking for help with estate planning, taxes, reading securities statements, understanding types of securities and the categories they belong in, and so much more. It's impossible to learn all the aspects of the financial world simply by taking a one- or two-year course.

Here's another reason. While clients may turn to a financial advisor for things such as estate planning and taxes, there are limits that the advisor must adhere to. For example, I teach estate planning at local colleges in my area. However, the actual estate plan must be drawn up by a lawyer. Regarding taxes, CPAs and other accounting experts will have knowledge and insight. But these individuals should work hand in hand with a financial advisor who fully understands the client's circumstance and situation as well as their unique needs. So, a wise financial advisor will have relevant experts as part of their team.

The lesson here is to *be careful!* Six to eight years of experience is the minimum needed, but I highly recommend finding someone with eight to ten years of experience when looking for your own financial advisor.

My Story

Here's my learning curve that I like to share with clients.

I ran a mortgage company in the late 1990s. During that time, I first was introduced to financial planning, which excited me, but I realized it would take money to switch gears into something I didn't know much about. However, my nature is to learn and consume information, so I spent about two years learning from top advisors in the financial planning industry and learning about investments. I've had extensive tax and estate planning experience and have sat with CPAs and top-notch attorneys who trained me on what I needed to know for financial planning. I'm the self-taught type, and my mortgage business allowed me to take the time to learn this industry.

After feeling that I had a solid start through my training, I started to meet with clients. However, after working in the industry for about five years, I found out that I could sign up to become a Chartered Financial Consultant (ChFC). When I consulted with some of my colleagues about taking this course, which is akin to taking an advanced degree in financial planning, they all told me the same thing: that given my acquired knowledge and experience, I had already learned the same concepts that are taught in this two-year course.

Typically, when a new advisor gets into this industry, the firm they work for pays for the advisor to obtain one of these certifications. At that point they have no experience and need to know the basics. So, whether an advisor has the necessary experience and if they are a fiduciary, a ChFC, or a CFP, there's not much difference among these three. What is necessary is that all three have a full understanding of taxes, estate planning, investment planning, and retirement planning and can provide these services to clients who may need some advice when it makes sense.

A Fiduciary Financial Advisor

Years ago, when I was determining when and how to enter the investment world, my research showed that the best fit for me was to become a fiduciary financial advisor, and here's why. A fiduciary advisor is a financial professional who is *legally* and *ethically* bound to act in the *best* interests of their clients. They must prioritize the needs of their clients above their own needs and financial gain, and they must always disclose any potential conflicts of interest. Fiduciaries who are financial advisors are subject to either federal or state regulation, including US Securities and Exchange Commission (SEC) oversight, meaning they are held to a higher standard.

When I earned my securities license, I wanted to be a fiduciary, which reflects who I am. I'm direct and straightforward.

Here's a good comparison.

Most people won't sell their own home because they can interfere with the actual sale. When you show the house yourself, you tend to be brutally honest with the prospective buyer. That honesty is admired but could also cost you the sale of that home. In the same way, a fiduciary should be brutally honest with you and give you the pros and cons of any plan or investment you are considering so that you can make the right decision. You want all your information up front so you don't find out something important after the fact.

Here are some other reasons why I became a fiduciary:

- In the financial world, in order to earn commissions, many professionals may have the incentive to sell certain products even if there are comparable products available at a lower price. However, fiduciaries are duty bound to seek the best prices and terms for their clients.

- Fiduciaries must thoroughly discuss all decisions with their clients, providing relevant information and pertinent facts, making it easier for the client to understand decisions regarding their assets and financial future.

- Every investment advisor registered with a US state or a state securities regulator must act as a fiduciary. Every registered advisor in that system operates on a fee-only basis.

How do you know if a financial advisor is a fiduciary? The Certified Financial Planners Board (CFPB), the Financial Industry Regulatory Authority (FINRA), and the National Association of Personal Financial Advisors (NAPFA) all have online search tools that make it easy to find fiduciaries in your area.

When you are looking for a fiduciary, it's important to get to know the individual *before* you do any investing. You can start by requesting a copy of their Form ADV[36] and Form CRS,[37] paperwork the SEC requires advisory firms to file. This will provide information about an advisor's business, pay structure, educational background, potential conflicts of interest, and disciplinary history. This informa-

---

36 Officially called the Uniform Application for Investment Adviser Registration and Report by Exempt Reporting Adviser. All investment advisors who manage more than $25 million must submit this registration document to the SEC and to state securities authorities.

37 This form contains a brief relationship summary to retail investors, including important information about a firm and key disclosures that can help you decide if a particular firm is right for you.

tion is also available online through the SEC's Investment Advisor Public Disclosure (IAPD) tool. You can also request a performance record and a list of client references to contact.

Here are some questions to ask an advisor you are vetting:

- "How do you earn your money?" An advisor may charge a flat fee, an hourly fee, or an asset-based fee, depending on the service being offered. Be sure to discuss any fees so you understand how they affect your portfolio.

- "What certifications and licenses do you hold?"

- "What services do you offer?" This question will help you determine if you want investment management or more comprehensive financial planning and wealth management services.

- "Do you specialize in clients based on a minimum investment?"

- "How often do you communicate with clients and in what method?" Find out if your fiduciary offers face-to-face meetings, phone calls, emails, or a combination of these, as well as how often these occur.

- "Can you provide a written guarantee of your fiduciary duty?"

- "Do you have any disclosures on your record?" It's important to know if an advisor or their firm has faced any past regulatory, criminal, or disciplinary actions or has violated rules or misled consumers.

- "What extra charge should I be made aware of?" Keep in mind that you might be responsible for trading and brokerage fees, fund fees, or extra charges such as implementing a financial plan created specifically for you.

- "What is your investment approach?" While some fiduciaries create customized portfolios according to an individual client's needs, others offer a selection of model portfolios. Also, fiduciaries can offer a range of risk levels and asset allocations based on the client's needs.

Robo-Advisors

Some companies are increasingly using robo-advisors, but this is something I have no interest in.

A robo-advisor is an automated digital platform that provides algorithm-driven financial advice and decisions. These platforms must hold a registration with the SEC. As an automated fiduciary, the platform is required to act in its client's best interests. However, robo-advisors have little to no human supervision, nor do they have any interaction with the outcomes of each account. This makes me question how an automated platform can offer the best individualized advice. Enough said.

A Top-Down Approach

The majority of my clients have a general need for income. They also want the income to be similar to their current employment income at a minimum. We also talk about additional income for the things they want to do while in retirement, such as travel or a new vehicle. When working with my clients, I create a "retirement risk report" to help each one determine their "need" goals and "want" goals.

It's the advisor's job to cover these goals correctly, or the client runs the risk of making an uneducated decision based on not having saved enough or, conversely, not having the assets needed to provide the income to enjoy retirement as they had hoped. Sadly, I've had people come to me who have spent money they didn't have during their go-go years and are at risk of running out of money by the time they make it to age eighty and beyond.

In my opinion, a top-down analysis is the most accurate way to determine the right income versus the bottom-up analysis, in which individuals try to evaluate all their expenses and end up missing particular aspects. We're creatures of habit; if our income increases at work, we adjust and increase our spending habits.

Here are three questions I ask each client regarding their money:

1. Did you save enough to make a big purchase like an RV, a second home, or a boat?

2. Did you save enough to leave your biggest inheritance to your children?

3. Did you maximize your income to meet all your goals while in retirement?

Of course, the third one is the most important one to answer, and this sets the stage to talk about income goals.

When working with a couple or an individual, we start with knowing their gross income, because this is what determines the lifestyle they have been accustomed to. The rule of thumb to determine the financial needs in retirement is as follows:

- Take the gross earned income that either the single person or the couple is earning.

- Reduce the amount by 25 percent. For example, if the total gross income is $100,000, then the adjusted income is $75,000. In most cases, this approach will take care of the basic needs in the individual's or couple's current lifestyle.

- Then we add back the amount of income needed to take care of the fun stuff in retirement. This is where retirees must be honest with themselves and not take shortcuts or underestimate the amount needed for retirement. With all that extra time on their hands, they're going to spend more than the basic needs.

Helping to Find the *Right* Advisor

When searching for investment help, keep in mind that not all financial advisors are created equal, even if that doesn't seem true to the average person. What I want to help you understand is that there's a difference between financial planning and working with a true retirement income specialist—in other words, what I call investing for income the old-fashioned way versus utilizing strategies today and hoping that the growth will be enough to carry you through all your retirement years.

Here are some questions to consider when interviewing a retirement financial advisor:

- "What type of clients do you work with primarily?"

- "Are at least 80 percent of your clients between fifty years old and eight-five years old?" That means the advisor works mainly with people in retirement and gives specific advice to a specific category of clients.

- "Do you use primarily prepackaged products such as mutual funds or exchange traded funds?" Many financial advisors use prepackaged products because it simplifies their internal processes, their administration, and their staff. While the products they offer might be diversified, they are not custom for each client.

- "I'm a moderate-risk investor (which represents 80 to 90 percent of most people). How do you determine the types of investment instruments that are best for me? How much income will my portfolio gain, and what is your investment strategy? What tools do you use to invest my money as a moderate-risk investor? How will income be generated? What types of allocations will be used?"

In my opinion, you want a financial advisor who is proactive with your retirement planning. As you probably know, the markets are cyclical, so you don't want a set-it-and-forget-it plan. When you're buying stocks and bonds with dividends and other similar instruments, you can react to the market's current cycle, be it bearish or bullish. In other words, you want to be moving in the direction that the economy warrants under different types of conditions. An astute advisor who is proactive will help you "buy low and sell high."

For example, a couple of years ago, energy stocks and bonds did very well for about ten months, and the majority of my clients were already invested to take full advantage of the run-up. Then there was a run-up in tech stocks. While no advisor can predict the future, an astute advisor has their hand on the pulse of the markets and can help their clients position themselves to take advantage of the next sector that will run up.

- "Do you primarily use mutual funds?"
  In my company, we call mutual funds the "disease of ease." Mutual funds are similar to prepackaged products, because the research has already been done. That may sound OK, but

mutual funds do not equate to a customized portfolio. They fall into the set-it-and-forget-it instruments.

- "How are you going to create income for my retirement?" Or put another way, "How much yield am I going to get on my portfolio, and is there a way you can show that to me?"

  This is important information to know, because in my company, we show clients what they're actually going to get prior to investing. We then meet with our clients on at least a quarterly basis so we can see that the "proof is in the pudding," so to speak. We want to make sure each client is getting enough yield to satisfy the income they need, so they don't have to worry about spending their principal early on.

Wrapping Up

Your money and how it is invested is the most important decision you can make. The return on your investments will have a direct impact on major areas of your life, such as where and how you live, the level of healthcare you receive, and the inheritance you leave. You want your retirement years to be truly "golden"! When choosing a financial advisor, be sure to interview more than one person. Find out who aligns with your values, goals, needs, and preferences, and above all, select the one you feel you can trust. Don't take shortcuts! Don't sell yourself short and regret your decision. Ideally, your financial advisor will be part of your life and will be there for your family after you leave this earth. You owe it to yourself and your family to do your research before signing with a financial advisor so that you are confident you're making the best hiring decision.

QUICK TAKES

- You should look for someone who primarily works with preretirees or retirees and is multifaceted in many areas to help you plan for your later years.

- When looking for a financial advisor, the key is to make sure they have been in business for eight to ten years at a minimum. Experience is everything.

- In my opinion, those who work for a bank or institution can take a cookie-cutter approach to their clients. Instead of getting to know each client individually and understanding their needs, they might put conservative clients in a couple of types of investment vehicles and progressive clients in a couple of different vehicles and then call it a day.

- Whether an advisor has the necessary experience and if they are a fiduciary, a CHFC, or a CFP, there's not much difference among these three. What is necessary is that all three have a full understanding of taxes, estate planning, investment planning, and retirement planning and can provide these services to clients who may need some advice when it makes sense.

- In my opinion, a top-down analysis is the most accurate way to determine the right income versus the bottom-up analysis, in which individuals try to evaluate all their expenses and end up missing particular aspects.

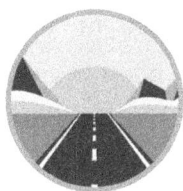

CONCLUSION

I wrote this book for one reason: to educate you, my reader, so that you are more aware and feel more confident when choosing and working with a financial advisor. It is commonly reported that Alan Greenspan, who served as the thirteenth chairman of the US Federal Reserve, noted that the number one problem in today's generation and economy is the lack of financial literacy. I completely agree. In my opinion, too many people blindly trust financial advisors, thinking these individuals know what they are doing and have the client's best interest in mind. However, in my opinion, too often they focus on what is best for the company they work for.

Here is something else to consider.

My experience tells me that the number one factor driving individuals to make the wrong financial decisions is that "money is emotional." Many times, people will go with their emotions over independent and objective decision-making during difficult times. While money is emotional, investing should be fact based and logical.

For these reasons and many more, the mission of Sparks Financial Group is to provide every client with financial confidence and peace of mind as we help them navigate the complexities of planning and saving for retirement. Our goal is to help ensure that every client can thrive—and not just survive—in their retirement years. My team and I recognize that everyone's goals for retirement are different, and once you enter retirement, your goals and dreams can change. That's why we take the time to get to know every client before creating their personalized financial plan. It's also why we take the time to conduct regular client reviews to help ensure that your financial plan continues to reflect your evolving goals and priorities.

In closing, no matter who you choose as your financial advisor, be sure they can help you identify your financial dreams and goals. That individual must have a clear understanding of your current financial situation and the direction you want to take so they can *objectively* use the best wealth management tools to customize a financial strategy designed to grow *your* wealth while protecting your assets. Over the life of your financial investing, you want someone who can offer valuable guidance, giving you peace of mind while supporting you to make informed decisions and achieve your financial goals.

ACKNOWLEDGMENTS

I want to thank God for his provisions and for making everything possible. He is always so far ahead of us and takes care of future unknowns and I'll trust him for the rest of my life.

I want to thank my wife, Debbie, for sticking with me through tough times, as well as many good times. She was there in full support of helping me to build our business to help retirees manage their financial affairs.

I want to thank my parents who were instrumental in encouraging me to think outside the box. They taught me work ethics and respect.

I want to thank Dave Scranton, Sound Income Group, and Retirement Income Source franchisees for supporting us and teaching us the fundamentals that focus on true retirement planning for our clients. Serving our clients in this capacity seems to me to provide less stress in their financial lives. We are making a difference and we look forward to many more years of service.

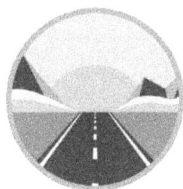

ABOUT THE AUTHOR

For nearly twenty years, Tim Sparks has helped families in the greater Lexington area achieve their financial and retirement goals.

Tim understands that seniors face many challenges when preparing for retirement. He created Sparks Financial Group, LLC to help retirees and preretirees manage the critical transition from asset accumulation to income distribution and preservation. Tim firmly believes that through financial education and conservative financial planning, he can help clients make informed decisions that better enable them to avoid costly mistakes, lower their tax liability, and increase the value of their estate.

Because Tim feels that financial education is so important, he is committed to providing educational workshops both in person and online. You can also hear him on his radio show, *The Retirement Income Show with Tim Sparks*, every weekend.

Tim serves as an Investment Advisor Representative for Sound Income Strategies, LLC, and as an independent life insurance agent. This allows him to bring a wide range of investment options to his clients.

Tim and his wife, Debbie, have a son and two daughters. They reside in Mt. Sterling, Kentucky. Leading his family to develop a strong Christian relationship is another one of Tim's top priorities.

CONTACT US

Sparks Financial Group

Sparks Financial Group is an independent financial planning firm with offices located in Lexington and Louisville, Kentucky. For nearly a decade, Sparks Financial Group has been dedicated to helping pre-retirees and retirees build strategies designed to protect and grow their assets ahead of and during retirement.

Our Mission

The mission of Sparks Financial Group is to provide every client with financial confidence and peace of mind as we help them navigate the complexities of planning and saving for retirement. Our goal is to help ensure that every client can thrive—and not just survive—in their retirement years.

We do this by helping each client identify their financial goals and dreams. Once we gain a clear understanding of your current financial situation and where you want to go, we'll use the best wealth management tools available to custom-tailor a personalized financial strategy designed to protect and grow your wealth.

For more information, contact the Sparks Financial Group

WEBSITE:
https://sparksfg.com

ADDRESS:
2285 Executive Drive, Suite 310,
Lexington, KY 40505

or

10200 Forest Green Boulevard, Suite 112,
Louisville, KY 40223

PHONE NUMBER:
(859) 273-1368

www.ingramcontent.com/pod-product-compliance
Lightning Source LLC
Chambersburg PA
CBHW031406180326
41458CB00043B/6629/J